# Making

*The Musician's Guide*

# Money

*to Cover Gigs*

# Making

*by Quint Randle and Bill Evans*

# Music

**Backbeat
Books**
San Francisco

Published by Backbeat Books
600 Harrison Street, San Francisco, CA 94107
www.backbeatbooks.com
email: books@musicplayer.com

An imprint of the Music Player Group
Publishers of *Guitar Player, Bass Player, Keyboard,* and other magazines
United Entertainment Media, Inc.
A CMP Information company

**CMP**
United Business Media

Distributed to the book trade in the US and Canada by
Publishers Group West, 1700 Fourth Street, Berkeley, CA 94710

Distributed to the music trade in the US and Canada by
Hal Leonard Publishing, P.O. Box 13819, Milwaukee, WI 53213

Text Design and Composition by Michael Cutter
Cover Design by Michael Cutter

Library of Congress Cataloging-in-Publication Data

Randle, Quint
Making money making music : a musician's guide to cover gigs / by Quint Randle and Bill Evans
   p. cm.
 ISBN 0-87930-720-X
Music—Vocational guidance. 2. Popular music—Economic aspects. I. Randle, Quint 1960- II. Title.

ML3795.R36 2002
780'.23'73—dc21

2002066722

Printed in the United States of America
02 03 04 05 06     5 4 3 2 1

*To my mom and dad, who were always there to listen.*
Quint


*To Gary Persons, who showed me how to find the right well.*
Bill

# Table of Contents

# PREFACE

Once upon a time in the music business, there were two groups of people who were responsible for making hit songs. These groups were known as writers and performers, and they very rarely overlapped. In fact, the idea of pop artists writing their own material was not even considered in most circles until rock & roll came along and broke all the rules. (In fact, even the Beatles' first album consists largely of songs written by others.)

That change in the early sixties set up a split that endures among bands even today, separating those that write their own material (sometimes called "original" bands, though very few are original in any way) from those who concentrate on interpreting and performing songs written and recorded by others. These bands are known—and in many corners derided—as "cover" bands.

This is a book about starting or joining a cover band. It was written by two guys who have been both dissed and envied by many of their fellow musicians for a couple of decades. Dissed because we both play in cover bands. Envied because we both actually get paid to play.

In the pages that follow we'll tell you about progressing and succeeding as a musician by performing cover material—that is, songs made popular by other artists—for fun and profit. For many, being in a cover band is not the end-all of being a musician; many players in cover bands have "original" projects on the side and may tell everyone that they just play covers until they "make it" with their own music.

The funny thing is that while bands performing their own songs are often more highly regarded by their friends and fans, most never make a dime playing music, while cover bands are in demand for high-paying corporate and private gigs, weddings, and club dates.

A wise man once said, "First you imitate, then you innovate." Playing covers, even if that is not your ultimate ambition, is a great way to learn the craft and art of performance. The discipline you gain learning and performing cover tunes will serve you well no matter where your musical adventures eventually take you. Whatever your eventual station in life as a musician, being in a cover band and playing cover material is an important step, a rite of passage along the way for virtually all big-time pro musicians.

In fact, the more we are around full-time pro musicians, the more we realize that playing covers remains an important activity even for those musicians good enough—and lucky enough—to spend most of their time recording and touring with well-known major label artists. Bill started the band he plays in now with a guitarist who has spent the last decade as the musical director for a major Nashville artist with four gold records and one platinum record to his credit, and Quint remembers doing sound for a band at a church dance where the stand-in guitarist dropped a few big names. (You never really know when to believe stories.) But a few weeks later he heard the guitarist's name being announced by Jackson Browne during a concert radio broadcast. And then a few months later he saw the guitarist playing "Back in the USSR" on MTV with Billy Joel in Russia. Yes, when "big-time" players are not on tour with their star employers, they're often playing the same kind of nightclub and private gigs you will read about in this book—the same type of gigs *you* will be playing.

Sometimes cover gigs are just a great way to have fun playing music and make a little money in the process. In some cases they can lead to much bigger things. Just ask Jorge Casas, whose gig at a South Miami bar led directly to a long-time gig with Gloria Estefan. Or ask David Santos, who made a connection playing a NYC wedding gig that led to a several-year gig with Billy Joel and from there to John Fogerty, the Neville Brothers, and Julio Iglesias. Or ask Skip Dorsey, who turned a Marriott Hotel Top 40 job into his gig as guitarist and musical director for pop megastar Britney Spears.

Or ask the two of us, who now in our 40s, continue to gig regularly while the same folks who dissed us back in high school gave up playing music years ago. We're not stars, but we're still having fun and we're still getting paid. And those are very cool things.

This book is set up in three sections: Sweat, Biz, and Tech. These are the three areas musicians must master to be successful, professional giggers. Check for more resources on the book's website: www.covergigs.com.

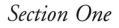

*Section One*

# Sweat

# FIRST STEPS TO GETTING STARTED

*You have to decide what the goals of your band are if you ever expect to achieve them. Not all bands and band members seek fame and fortune, which is good because relatively few ever see it.*

Dr. George Marakas

Like most good things in life, being in a band requires a lot of preparation. We're not saying it's like going to college or law school, but "learning to play" an instrument is just the beginning of the process. On the other hand, one of the most stifling things any musician can do is to avoid playing in performing situations, opting instead for endless hours of solitary practice. You've got to strike a balance between personal perfection and public performance. You can practice forever, trying to master your particular instrument, but you can never really master it until you are performing for an audience on a regular basis. Luckily, many musicians have this inherent drive to perform for an audience. If you're not one of those folks, you're going to have to learn how to force yourself. Although he was known primarily as a studio guitarist, the late Tommy Tedesco made just that point in his book, *For Guitar Players Only*: "As a youth, form your own band. No matter how bad it is, it will get better. Start playing jobs as early as possible. Money–no object. Learn, learn, learn."

## What do you need to know?

Ask 100 giggers this question and you'll likely get about as many different answers. In fact, that's exactly what we did. And here's a sample of what we heard:

*The first thing a beginning gigger should be able to do is play their instrument in the appropriate style and tempo of the music of the band they're joining. As a bandleader, I can deal with someone who's inarticulate, but I can't deal with an incompetent.*

Kevin Johnsrude

*We found the most important item for a starting group was compatible personalities. Even then, there are times when personalities clash. Many other things come into play, but if you do not get along you will never go very far.*

Paul Lenig

*The three most important elements for someone to be a successful gigger are honesty, commitment, and business sense.*

Malcolm Hunter

*I think a major thing giggers should know is that the people who are there to see you perform don't have to be there. These people have chosen to be there, and because of that, you (as a gigger and a courteous person) should do the best you can to make them welcome. It's not always the best musician who wins over the crowd. Sometimes it's the musician who treats his or her audience the best instead.*

Fritz Scherz

*If you don't understand the basics of music and chord theory, you're going to feel like you're in a foreign country where you can't speak the language.*

Ken Carver

## The basics

The one thing most of us agree on (and something that virtually every gigger we spoke with agreed on) is that any potential gigger should have at least some grasp of music terminology. This is not to say that you have to become some kind of music theory geek, but you should at least be able to communicate with other musicians in a common language.

Marty Jourard played sax and keyboards in the L.A.-based, New Wave band the Motels, recording four records with the band and co-writing one of the band's biggest hits, "Take The L," as well as "Total Control," which was later covered by Tina Turner. He also wrote a magazine column called Practical Theory for three years. Marty is a rock & roll guy, but he still knows how music works: "So many musicians have this weird attitude about music theory, as if some unnamed magic will disappear when they learn to identify the chord they're playing. It's fun to know what the hell you're doing."

You may get an opportunity to join a band before you really know any of this technical music stuff, and that's fine. Take the plunge. Just be prepared to do some cramming to keep up. You'll have to fake it until the real stuff arrives. Both Quint and Bill started bands long before they knew much more than how to play a barre chord. In some recently aired interviews with U2, Bono and the Edge talked about how they didn't even know how to play their instruments when they first started the band—they just wanted to start a band. And that's all that really mattered for them. But the key word here is "started." When *you* start a band, you can get away with a lot—at least for a while. But if you are looking to join an established band, you need to have a grasp of the basics of music communication and competency.

At minimum, you should be able to read a chord chart, understand the concept of keys, be familiar with the time signatures common in pop music (4/4, 3/4, 6/8, and maybe 12/8), and have at least a rudimentary understanding of common chord progressions. (I-IV-V, ii-V-I, and I-vi-IV-V come immediately to mind.) As you learn an increasing number of classic cover songs, you'll begin to recognize the various basic chord progressions. And some musical genres—like country and the blues—rely more heavily on basic chord progressions.

Not knowing the basics can lead to problems that range from hurt feelings to band breakups. An example: About a dozen years ago, Bill started working in a typical rock band with a singer, a drummer, and a bass player. After some time spent rehearsing—and just a week and a half before their first gig—the group decided they needed to round out the sound a bit and brought in another guitar player. This guy played pretty well, sang really well, and was a whiz at MIDI sequencing, which eventually allowed the band to add keyboard and horn sounds without adding additional players. But the band almost never got to that point.

In trying to prepare for that debut gig, the band had to double the size of its set list and do it quickly. The band members had all been playing in bands long enough to know plenty of "standard" rock songs—enough to get them through a local bar gig without problems. All of them, that is, except the new guitar player. The bandleader would call out a tune, something simple by the Stones or maybe Chuck Berry, and they would decide on a key and get ready to run through it. The new guitarist would say, "I don't know it." Then Bill would reassure him by saying something like, "Don't worry, it's just a I-IV-V in E."

It was hot in the rehearsal space, and they had been at it for several hours. Things were getting tense. The new guy was struggling, but the band was plowing forward anyway. Time was short. Finally, after going through the process outlined above a number of times, he exploded. "What in the hell are you talking about?" he yelled. "What the hell is a IV?"

Even after you know the basics, you have to take stock of your abilities before accepting a gig. Not doing so can lead to disaster. Here's another example: A couple of years ago, Bill got a call to play on a series of Christmas concert gigs for a local church. He figured the bread was pretty good, they were only asking for one session before dress rehearsal, and the music was original musical theater-type stuff for a local church. How hard could it be? Long story short, the church's musical director was a serious composer and the music was hard—not beyond Bill's ability to play, but well beyond his ability to read. He got through it, but just barely, and he never got another call from that group.

## Assessing your strengths and weaknesses

In addition to making sure you really know this music theory stuff, you must also assess your abilities in several other areas. The two basic musical areas are instrument and vocals. On the business side, the areas are selling and networking.

The real question you need to ask yourself in assessing your strengths is, "What am I *really* bringing to the party?" Pick *one* thing you do really well. Are you a quality lead guitarist who can sing great backup vocals? Or are your backup vocal abilities only marginal? Are you a great vocalist who can play strong second guitar? Sure, you'll need to fill many roles in a cover band, but you have to know what your real value is. Your real strength may not even be musical: You may be a great leader or great at making connections and landing gigs. Quint has never been the greatest player in the world; he's a pretty strong vocalist, but plenty of players out there are much more talented and more committed to their art. Quint realized long ago—after some wise advice from his older, recording engineer brother—that his greatest strength was in organizing and leading other musicians.

(Don't feel too bad if you aren't musically accomplished yet. We've all heard the stories of bands starting, and so-and-so getting asked to join because he or she owned a real PA system. If that's your ticket into the group, then go for it!)

But that is not an easy thing for most of us to do. It's hard to take an honest look at ourselves. So in addition to evaluating yourself, you may want to invite an objective third party to critique your skills. One word of advice: This objective third party should probably not be a spouse or significant other; many times they can be overly positive—or negative—about your skills. "Oh, you're the greatest guitarist that ever lived. I'll come to all your gigs," says the classic groupie girlfriend (who needs to get a life). On the other side of the coin, a longtime partner can be your harshest critic. Both are sometimes "too close" to see your true strengths and weaknesses. So find someone outside your inner circle whom you respect musically.

### Identifying your musical direction

Just because you're playing music made famous by others doesn't mean you can play *everything* that *anyone* has made famous. The days of bands-as-living-jukeboxes have been over for a long time. You have a much better chance of getting gigs if you specialize in a style or era. Do a tribute band. Capitalize on your strengths and focus on a genre where you can literally play to those strengths. For example, if your strengths are basic rhythm guitar and vocals, you may want to join some type of an oldies band where these skills are featured prominently.

In short, identifying your musical direction means searching within yourself and finding a direction that fits your musical tastes as well as the realities of your talents and the interests of the public.

## Master 30-40 songs

After you've decided on your musical direction or a genre you want to concentrate on, the next thing you've got to do—if you haven't done so already—is learn and memorize at least 30-40 songs. We're talking no lead sheets, cheat sheets, etc. These are songs you need to know inside and out, up and down. You have to be able to play and sing them in your sleep—the entire song, not just the cool solo. If you play and sing backup, learn the backup vocal parts as well. Depending on the genre, about half should be newer tunes—no more than five years old. The other half should be older, or songs considered classics from that genre. Why? We've both found that when auditioning players or auditioning for a band, only about half of what you know already will apply to the new band. A basic repertoire of 30-40 songs gives you a basic foundation from which to draw, grow, and progress. These 30-40 songs from any particular genre will also give you a musical vocabulary through which you can communicate with other musicians. You can use some of the tips found in Chapter 4, later in this section, to help you decide what songs to learn.

## The personal demo

After you've mastered the songs you are focusing on, you'll want to choose about five of them that showcase the best of your abilities. Then, from those songs, pick the best sections and record a personal demo. Why? Because you could waste hours and hours driving around town (especially in large cities like L.A. or Chicago) to auditions that waste your time and the time of those whom you're looking to play with. A personal demo will save that time and present your talents in a professional manner. The best sections might be a verse and chorus of one song, followed by the intro and first verse of another song, followed by the bridge and final chorus of another song, etc. It does not have to be anything fancy. Don't go into an expensive studio, but don't use a little portable recorder either. You can record it on a basic computer-based home recording system—Cakewalk's Guitar Studio for example (available for less than $50).

This personal demo should feature your raw abilities—just you and the microphone. Of course, if you are strictly a vocalist, you can either hire a musician, or use some quality karaoke tracks to back you up, provided they're in a key that's comfortable for you. (Priddis

Music, for example, has more than 1,500 songs in its catalog at www.priddis.com.)

Once you've got a demo you can be proud of, you're ready to put yourself out on the market. This is true whether you're trying to join a band or trying to form one. If you find an interesting opportunity, ask if you can send them your personal demo. Be sure to add, "If you like what you hear, we can get together if it feels right." In addition to saving time, this will also save you from putting yourself in embarrassing situations.

How do you find these opportunities? We're getting to that ... but first, a few words on another tool that can increase the odds of finding what you want.

## Learning to read

We've already touched on the importance of learning chord charts and lead sheets. Now let's move ahead to the idea of reading actual music notation. You know—notes. In eras past, this would not have been optional: Musicians learned how to read music as a natural part of learning their instrument. But in the rock era many players—especially those playing the rock staples of guitar, bass, and drums—are self-taught, and many players, even some pro-level folks touring with big-name acts, cannot read music. So if you don't know how to read music, should you take the time to learn?

It depends on what you want to do in your musical endeavors and how far you want to take it. The other variable is the kind of music you are playing. Most guys in rock bands don't read. Ditto for country and a lot of singer-songwriter types. If you are playing jazz, though, you will be expected to be able to at least follow a lead sheet. And theater gigs and most serious recording gigs demand serious reading chops.

Not all rock band guys are notationally illiterate. As the drum columnist for *Gig* magazine, Dave Beyer has written a couple of times about how being able to read and write a very simple chart has helped him get and keep good gigs. Here is what he had to say a few years back in *Gig*:

■　■　■

Once upon a time—actually at about 7 p.m.—a drummer buddy (D.B.) of mine got a call from the tour manager of a very well-known rock artist. The manager asked D.B. if he was interested in auditioning for an upcoming tour. Naturally, D.B. said, "Yes." The manager said, "Great, show up tomorrow at 10 a.m., and by the way, learn the first eight songs on the current CD."

Upon returning from the record store, D.B. sat down at the drums, popped the headphones on, and started to learn the songs. After he had memorized the first song's drum patterns, the stops, the tricky part in the middle, and the ending, an hour-and-a-half had passed. At this rate, he would have all eight songs ready to go by 9 the next morning, leaving just enough time for a quick shower and five cups of coffee. But after staying up all night, he'd probably suck and not get the gig.

There's gotta be a better way, D.B. thought. Then he flashed back to a drum lesson he'd had years ago, when his teacher taught him how to write his own drum charts. He recalled the concepts: song form, how to transcribe a drum beat, how to use measure and section repeat signs, and how to count bars; but most important, how to quickly get it all down on paper, saving countless hours of memorization time. If there was ever a time to put chart-writing skills to work, it was now. D.B. grabbed some music paper and a pencil, and got down to business.

He began by listening to an entire song while writing down the form or sections that make up the tune. It started with an intro, which was followed by a verse. Next came the chorus, followed by another verse and chorus. Then there was a part that sounded different from the verse and chorus, which was the bridge. After that came two more choruses and an ending section (sometimes called the outro).

D.B. got the form down in one listen. After writing the order in the top left corner of his music paper, he was ready to write a more complete drum chart. He remembered his teacher explaining the next step, to count the measures or bars in each section: 1-2-3-4, 2-2-3-4, 3-2-3-4, 4-2-3-4, and so on. The intro was four bars long. Using the same counting method for the rest of the song, D.B. noted eight-bar verses, eight-bar choruses, a four-bar bridge, and a four-bar outro.

Next he wrote the names of the sections in the left hand margin of the chart. That way with a quick glance he could see what was coming up. Then he wrote the drum pattern (or beat) in the first bar of each section, and used measure repeat signs (✗) to tell him to keep repeating that pattern through the remaining bars in that section. Also to save writing time and space, he used section repeat signs at either end of the repeating choruses.

Instead of taking the time to transcribe the actual drum fills, he wrote the word "fill" over the bars where they occurred. He knew in the heat of battle he would just play a spontaneous fill, anyway.

Since it always pays to follow the singer (especially when they're paying you), D.B. wrote the lyrics under the first few bars of each section. That way, if the singer jumped to the bridge early, he'd be ready.

After a couple more listens, D.B. had the chart down. By repeating the process for all eight tunes, and allowing about 10 or 15 minutes to play along with each song, he was done and thoroughly prepared in four hours, and in bed by midnight.

On the way to the audition the next morning, D.B. recalled his teacher stressing the golden rule of using your own drum charts on a gig or at an audition: *Play the music, not the chart.* Keep the chart low and relatively out of sight. Use it as a reference without staring at the page, and play the tune with confidence and conviction.

D.B. did just that. How does the story end? With a confession. D.B. is not really my drumming buddy; he's me, Dave Beyer. And my chart-writing skills paid off. I got the gig with Melissa Etheridge, and it turned into an amazing three-year tour.

■ ■ ■

Dave's ability to create and read simple charts was key to nailing that audition, and the gig was an important turning point in his musical career. But even in the world of the local cover band, not being able to read can cause problems. For example, if your group includes horns or a keyboard player, those folks likely read. If you don't, it can lead to some difficulties in rehearsal situations when the leader says to pick the tune up at "section B" or "bar 64", and you are wondering which verse he or she means. Not knowing how to read should not stop you from getting out there and playing, but it is something you should at least try to learn. If nothing else, the discipline can't hurt.

## The bottom line

So if you have acquired some basic reading and playing skills, identified your niche, learned 30 songs by heart—and you still have the heart—you may have what it takes to head out into the big bad world of being a semi-professional musician. You just might be able to land yourself in a real band, or start one. So let's turn the page and get ready to rock and roll.

**SWEAT 2**

# JOINING A BAND

*For any starting-out gigger, a clear understanding of the kinds of music the band will be playing, and where the band will be playing that music, is even more important than a grasp of musical terminology. If he/she wants to play the blues in various blues bars where people sit and listen appreciatively, and the rest of the band wants to play party tunes at private parties where people are up and dancing and having a rowdy ol' time, then you have a fundamental source of friction right from the get-go.*

Phil Raymondo

Wouldn't it be great if you could just go out and join the right band—one that's just waiting for your call? One that has a great reputation and plays exactly the kind of music you liked? Maybe even has an agent? And above all, is gigging regularly for good money? Sure, this is sort of a pipe dream, but it could actually happen. So before you go through the process of starting your own band from scratch, consider going out and joining an existing band—at whatever level.

Quint was able to do this a number of years ago. He answered an ad on a campus bulletin board; a cover band was looking for a lead vocalist. And while the band wasn't gigging yet, the players and talent were there. They were just looking for the one missing link. After about a month of heavy practicing, they were doing their first paying gigs and marketing themselves to a variety of venues.

### Pros and cons

While there are a lot of advantages to joining an existing band—mainly time and money—there are disadvantages as well. For example, an existing band will more likely than not have its leadership in place. By that we mean there will be a power structure and hierarchy for making decisions about what songs to play, what gigs to take, etc. There may be personality clashes you simply don't see during auditions. It's like any new job; you never really know how much you're going to like it until you've worked there for a month or so. The group may have also invested heavily in band-owned PA equipment, and you will either have to buy in or be paid by the band as sort of a hired gun or freelancer. But in most instances, the advantages of not having to go through the growing pains of putting a band together far outweigh the disadvantages of joining an established band—if you can find the right group of players.

### Finding the right band

With your personal demo in hand, a growing list of songs in your personal set list, and some music communication skills, you're ready to go out and find that group or band. You have several options when trying to find a group to join, and you should employ all of them. These include word-of-mouth contacts, placing an ad in a local music or entertainment paper, and posting a flier at a local music store or school campus, or on the Internet.

Word of mouth is a great way to find a band if you're a known player in your area. But the chances of that happening are slim to none if you're not. We've all heard the stories of how big-name bands seem to grow out of competing bands losing and swapping players. But even if you're not a known player, mention to people that you are looking to join a band. Tell your music teacher. Tell anybody who will listen. Give people your business card. Give them a piece of paper with your phone number on it. Anything. Word gets around—even in a big town. As á novice you are likely to find a partially formed band through this method—a group of players who are just a bit more organized than you are at the moment.

### Writing an ad

If you decide to place an ad in a paper or a flier at a music store, take the time to write the right kind of ad. You need to strike a balance between piquing the interest of bands looking for players and coming off as an egomaniac. Rule No. 1 is to keep it short and to the point. This is not the place to get into an extended discussion of your musical influences and stylistic faves. Following is a sample ad a guitarist might post on an index card or in the classified section of a newspaper. Take a look at it, then we'll dissect it for important key words.

Guitarist/vocalist looking for working or soon-to-be working cover band. Able to play many styles including rock, blues, R&B, and current pop. Sing backup and some lead. Pro gear. Reliable transportation. No drugs or egos. Serious only. 555-5555.

Let's take a look at this from the top. By starting with the term *guitarist/vocalist*, you are letting potential band mates know up front that you can and, more important, are willing to sing. This makes you twice as valuable as the player who can't or won't sing right from the beginning. Next, look at the terms *working or soon-to-be working*. This says you are looking for gigs—paying gigs. And if "working" doesn't do it, the inclusion of the words *cover band* will weed out the hundreds of rock star wannabe's that populate the rehearsal studios and music stores in most good-size towns.

*Able to play many styles* lets them know you are not a "one-riff wonder" who says "I only play (fill in then blank with anything from speed metal to polkas)." The line *sing backup and some lead* qualifies the opening guitarist/vocalist line and should set lead vocalists at ease that you are not out to take their gig. *Pro gear* is a crucial phrase, but you had best be able to back it up. We'll go into specifics for different players in the Tech section of this book, but suffice it to say that a battered guitar with noisy volume pots and a 12-watt practice amp don't qualify. *Reliable transportation* shows them you can get to rehearsals and gigs. *No drugs or egos* implies that you will cause no problems with either. *Serious only* says that you are just that. You'll also want to consider including your age, or the age range of band mates you are willing to work with (although, the type of music you are playing usually gives this away).

If you are posting a flier, then you have more room than you'd have on a card. Still, keep the copy focused. Make it look organized and professional. Don't scratch "Musician looking to jam" on some torn notebook paper and tack it on the bulletin board. Type it up and print it out on a 3x5 sheet of paper or a notecard. Look for this same type of professionalism and focus when reading ads and announcements you may want to respond to. At various times in our careers we have spent hours driving all over the greater Los Angeles area, going to auditions for bands we later wished had done a better job of representing themselves in their ads or fliers. Save yourself and others a lot of time by creating and responding to the right kind of musicians-seeking-musicians ads.

## Asking the right questions

When you call, or someone calls you, you need to know how to ask the right questions so you don't waste your time. This strategy, combined with your personal demo tape, will go a long way toward ensuring that you don't join a band that is wrong for you. It will also save you from a lot of wasted driving time and frustrating auditions.

That initial phone call is the band's first impression of you. It's also your chance to feel out the job and decide if it's something you really want to do. Some people will go on any audition they can, with the idea that even if it's not for them, they might make a contact that could result in future work. But really, it's not fair to waste a group of people's time if you know that the gig just isn't your style.

While you're being interviewed, ask questions yourself. Commitment issues, like rehearsal and travel expectations, music style, and performance style are important when deciding if you even want to audition for a band. Ask questions up front, before the audition, but don't come off sounding like an egomaniac either. If you ask too many questions they may perceive you to be a prima dona. Still, ask where they're playing, how much money they're making, and how they choose their material. Listen hard to what's being said, and if it's not for you, don't audition.

Here are some of the questions you can expect to be asked in an initial phone call.

## What kind of experience do you have?

This is a tough one when you are just starting out. As in any other career, it's always easier to find a job in music when you already have one. The challenge here is to present yourself in as positive a light as possible without flat-out lying. With that in mind, your answer should never be "none." Be creative: That open mic night can count as a gig, and the guys you have been jamming with can be a "local band." Try to make up for what you lack in experience with enthusiasm and a positive attitude. Let the interviewer know you're not afraid of hard work.

Be specific. Some people might interpret, "I play rhythm guitar" to mean that you don't play guitar very well. But an answer like, "I'm sort of like a Tom Petty-ish rhythm guitarist" means something totally different.

## What kind of music do you listen to?

This question can tell the interviewer a lot about you musically. It can also pigeonhole you way too quickly. It's important to be honest here. Don't say you love System of a Down because they were mentioned in the ad if your personal tastes run more to dance pop than metal. It's also important to be specific, even if you have wide-ranging tastes. "Everything" is a lousy answer. "Everything from Nine Inch Nails to Lee Ann Womack" is much better.

## What kind of an image do you have?

This is the polite way to ask, "What do you look like?" It's a hard truth for those of us who aren't model-types, but image is important to most bands, and many have a very specific look in mind. It helps to do some homework. If you know the band goes for leather and piercings, then don't call if you're not comfortable with that.

## Do you have reliable transportation?

This will be more important in some locales than others, but it can be *hugely* important. The band needs to know that you can get to gigs and rehearsals without a problem. Unless you can carry your gear without a dolly, and your town has great all-night public transportation, you need to consider a car as part of your personal rig and keep it maintained just as consistently.

## Successful auditioning

Knowing how to audition is obviously crucial if you are trying to join a working band. To close this chapter, we asked several working giggers for insights into the auditioning process.

Trumpeter Bill Churchville has auditioned for and played with a list of artists that includes Clint Black, Shakira, and Billy Joel; one audition led to a six-year stint with Tower of Power. Following are his audition tips, presented in timeline form.

■ ■ ■

### Two weeks before the audition

- Make a list of all the songs the band performs live. Ask if they have live tapes available.
- Compile a work tape of the songs you've chosen. Include a couple of songs that the band doesn't usually perform live—songs you'd have difficulty playing if they popped up at the audition.
- Start playing the work tape in your home, car, etc. Get the sound and the feel of the music in your head. Practice the songs; remember that it's better to do a little bit each day than to try to cram at the last minute. Get the notes under your fingers. Try to capture the feel of the music, in addition to playing the right notes.
- Brush up on the band's history. It may come in handy. If you know someone who's played in the group before, call and ask questions about the gig. Does the band pay on time? What's it like working with the leaders? Why is a spot opening up?

### One week before

- You should be thoroughly familiar with the music by now, but continue with your daily practice schedule.
- Check in with your band contact and start thinking about wardrobe; the idea is to look like you belong in the band. If they wear leather and chains onstage, don't audition in a tuxedo.
- If your chops don't get going until after noon, try to schedule your audition time accordingly.
- If possible, set your audition at the end of the process. Usually the first few people to audition set the grade for the rest. If you come in at the end of the process and you really burn, your performance will stay in the band members' minds (and ears).

### Three days before

- Practice with endurance in mind, to make sure that you don't run out of gas—you never know if the band will want to hear several tunes or even a short set.

- Organize and practice the tunes in order, as if you were playing a gig. Stand up, jump around—do everything you would normally do in performance. You want to duplicate the band's physical intensity as much as possible.

## Two days before
- Play through your set in front of a mirror or video camera, and be conscious of your stage presence.
- Work with the wardrobe. The idea is to look great but to also be as comfortable as possible. You'll have enough stress from the audition process without having to deal with uncomfortable clothes.
- Ask a friend with a good sense of style to critique your wardrobe, and have a musician friend you respect critique your performance.
- Think about job interview questions you may be asked about your résumé and musical influences.
- Prepare a few questions of your own, but try not to talk too much about business until you have an offer. You don't want to lose the gig before it's offered.

## The day before
- Think about what kind of attitude you want to project. These days it's not enough to be a great player; a group wants to know if you can get along with others—especially after three weeks on a tour bus in mid-January in the upper Midwest.
- Play through your set again. Don't hit it too hard.
- Get plenty of sleep.

## The day of the audition
- Do a light warm-up. Resist the temptation to practice. If you don't have the music down by now, practicing today is not going to help.
- Eat light.
- Give yourself plenty of time to get to the audition early.
- Be confident. Relax, you've done the homework. You've anticipated just about everything. It's normal to be nervous. Try to channel the nervous energy into positive energy.
- Breathe.
- Expect to have to read. Expect to be surprised at least once. If

asked to play an improvised solo, remember to play the idiom.
Don't play Coltrane changes on an R&B solo.

• Remember, everybody there hopes you are the one. They want you
to be good. Have fun. Play your best. Be sure to thank the band
for their time and their consideration.

### The morning after

Leave this day open in case they call you back for a second audition. Call your contact and thank him or her for the audition. Resist
the temptation to go out and spend all of the money that you will
soon be making after you get your new gig.

If you get the gig... great! If you don't, ask yourself, "What can I
learn from this?" and "What can I do to be better next time?" Then,
chalk it up to experience. Try to do as many auditions as possible
because every one is different. Every one you do makes you more
confident and relaxed. So when that dream gig comes along, you'll
already have several auditions under your belt. Good luck and happy
hunting.

Debra Davis has shared the stage with artists ranging from Edwin
McCain to Stephen Bishop to Gov't Mule. She also has two of her
own CDs out and has placed her songs in several movies and TV
shows. Debra knows that what makes an audition successful is confidence. Here's what she says:

Whether auditioning for a part in a musical or to be Madonna's
background singer, you might encounter flocks of people in line
vying for the same role you seek. This is called a "cattle call." It's
often associated with acting but certainly applies to music as well.
Sitting in a waiting area of singers or players being ushered in and
out as if by number can be unsettling, so the first thing you have to
tackle in auditioning is keeping your head on straight.

It's okay to have butterflies; the key is getting them to fly in for-
mation. Whatever your favorite ritual or mode of relaxing and finding focus, do that. But also breathe deep, and don't check out everyone else there and compare yourself to them; concentrate instead on

your strong points and above all, be prepared. The only thing you should be thinking about is knocking their socks off, not worrying, "Will I remember the words?"

Dress the part. If you don't fit the description of what *they* have in mind, you may be disqualified, even if you do have the talent. You wouldn't want to go to a country band audition dressed like Marilyn Manson or vise versa. Good way to get a "Next!"

When it's time to strut your stuff, go in with a smile, show confidence but not cockiness, and let it rip. Deliver the goods with as much enthusiasm and emotion and conviction as you would in a real performance. Make eye contact with the judges or the band-leader or the onlookers. At the end of your song or songs, thank them, shake hands if possible, and leave with head held high. Even if you make a flub or two, it's the overall impression that counts.

Finally, don't torture yourself and go out for things you really know you're not cut out for. Be realistic. But if you are in the right ballpark, don't give up if you strike out a few times. It toughens the skin a little, and helps you build up and perfect your auditioning chops until you hit the home run.

■ ■ ■

Cheryl Evans is another gigger with a ton of experience. She is currently the lead vocalist in two popular cover bands—Up All Nite and 80's Flashback. She starts with some advice on what to bring to an audition:

■ ■ ■

Bring your own song list. Type a neat, clean list of songs you know well, and the key you perform them in. Include the artist who does the original, since some songs have similar names that can lead to confusion. Put your name and phone number on the sheet, make copies, and prepare to leave one with the auditioner when you're done. Consider a personal promo pack: A single sheet, 8x10 head-shot on one side w/contact info and a short bio on the back, works well. Include instruments played and equipment you own. Have this multi-printed, and make sure it looks pro. If you have a personal demo, you can include it in your presentation.

As to the actual audition, don't walk into an audition and immediately start making excuses about not being warmed up or prepared, or why your equipment is screwed up, or receiving your audition music at the last minute. No one wants to hear that; it will almost certainly get you a "Thanks for coming" and no callback.

Don't show up late. If you can't show up on time for the audition, what's to make them believe you won't show up late for the international flight to Tahiti for that weekend gig? That being said, it's okay to show up a few minutes early, but not a lot more than that. Everyone can get uncomfortable when too many auditionees show up at once. Being too early can raise your own anxiety level while you listen to others ahead of you.

Cheryl told us she once went to audition for a very successful cover band with a house gig. But so did seemingly every other female vocalist in L.A. They told them all to get there at the same time, so a roomful of girls had to listen to every one else ahead of them. The anxiety level was so high in that room that nobody was doing well, and everyone was just waiting for a major cat fight to break out.

Don't come on too cocky. Be humble. Let your playing show your confidence.

Don't stand there fiddling with your equipment. Make sure your gear works before you go into the audition. Do keep in mind that great bands are like a great sports team. They're looking for a team player. So be a team player.

# SWEAT 3

# STARTING YOUR OWN BAND

*Research your area for what kinds of bands are getting the gigs, and ask if there is a void in the marketplace that needs to be filled, or if it is a void because no one is interested in that particular sort of band. As an example of what I mean, here in Minneapolis we have a band that is making tons of money playing disco music live, rather than by a DJ. They found a void and capitalized on it.*

Michael Boylen

Even with all the hard work and potential pitfalls, there are several good reasons for someone to start his or her own band. The most obvious one is that you are a leader, a self-starter; you like to be in control of your destiny. You're the same type of person who would be self-employed, not the type of person who likes to punch the clock. We're not talking about being a control freak, but let's face it, when you put a band together you get to take a greater part in directing things and help the band stay focused. (Read: Play *your* kind of music!)

But there are other reasons that someone would start a band instead of joining one.

Let's suppose you've gone through all the steps in Chapter Two, but with no success. This may have nothing to do with you or your talent; it may have to do with the market conditions in your area. You may be a great player, but there just may flat-out not be a band to join. So if your desire is great enough to perform for a live audience, then you're going to want to start your own band. And if you're a performer, more than just a musician (like we talked about in Chapter One), then that desire will be there.

Another reason why you may not be able to find a band is that—let's be honest—you're just not good enough. When bands are auditioning players, they have the cream of the crop to choose from; you just may have been down a notch or two from the other players. But that doesn't mean you shouldn't try to start a band. Quint has never been in a band he didn't somehow start; he has never got a gig auditioning for a band that wasn't in its infancy. He's a better than average player and singer, but he's mainly a good leader, organizer, and promoter. As for Bill, the couple of times he has joined a band he did not start have been less than satisfying experiences. So if you have the basic skills and the drive, but just can't find a band that appreciates you, then you may have to start one yourself.

Speaking of appreciation, there is one other reason why you may not have been able to find a band to join: Your musical vision may be significantly different from what's out there in the marketplace. It may be that "your" kind of band just doesn't exist. Your concept is so fresh and new that *you and only you* will be able to create it. Who would have thought that a cover band doing Led Zeppelin songs in a reggae style with a lead singer dressed up as Elvis would have been a commercial success. But that's just what happened with Greg Tortell (a.k.a. Tortelvis) and the band Dread Zeppelin.

### Finding and filling a musical niche

Whether conventional or bizarre, it's important to find your musical niche. "Understand what the market is for your band, and how you will reach that market," says Rollin Riggs, manager of the Bouffants and the Venus Mission.

That's the hard truth: Just because you like a certain set of tunes, there is no guarantee that anyone will want to listen. The trick is to find a musical niche that you—and potential audiences in your area—can dig.

### The easy way

Most bands have traditionally followed the path long traveled by Top 40 bands. By playing very current music and turning their set list over every couple of months, these bands found it unnecessary to fit into a unique niche. But, as rap and heavily produced dance pop grew to dominate radio fare, these gigs became the near-exclusive domain of the DJ. Bands that wanted to compete had to move past just providing music and go with some kind of entertainment hook that helps them stay booked.

Jerry Cobb and Cheryl Evans, a husband-and-wife team, have fronted a popular Top 40 band in Southern California called Up All Nite for the better part of two decades. At some point in the mid-'90s, they noted an increase in audience demand for some of the songs they played as Top 40 hits in the '80s. Problem was, doing too many of those older songs would confuse bookers who thought they were hiring a current cover band. So Jerry and Cheryl launched a side project—a costumed act called '80s Flashback. That side project eventually became their main band, with more work than they could get with Up All Nite.

Another band we covered in the pages of *Gig*—from the Miami, Florida, area—took another path, incorporating high-tech lighting and dance steps into the act and making sure that their lead singer wore outfits that were extremely revealing and sensual.

The common thread here is that both of these successful bands moved beyond the music to find and fill a unique niche in their market. Even in a Top 40 band, where the songs you play are largely dependent on what is on the *Billboard* charts, there are tricks to picking the right songs. (More on this in the following chapter.)

## Where to look for players

All the same advice and tips offered in the previous chapter apply here as well. You've got a variety of places to hang fliers, place ads, or otherwise spread the word, ranging from the local music store to the Internet to word of mouth. The more specific you are in describing the type of player(s) you are looking for, the fewer phone calls you are going to have to field and the less time you will waste. So write a very descriptive ad and get it out in as many places as possible. One word of caution: Don't be too descriptive, or you may not get any phone calls at all.

## Running an audition

Knowing what a band is about is crucial to maintaining it over the long haul. In the same sense, knowing what you are looking for before starting the audition process is crucial to your success. If you plan on doing songs heavy on the vocal harmonies, then hiring non-singing players is not a great way to go, no matter how well they play.

The best way to keep sight of what you need may be to make a list and let that be your guide during auditions. Riley Wilson advocates just such an approach in a piece he did on auditioning and came up with a list that looks like this:

■ ■ ■

**Drummer:** Solid time, ability to swing, chart reader, quick study, versatile, stylist, good "feel" player, etc.
**Bassist:** Solid time, able to play different styles, reader, doesn't overplay, quick study, good ear, etc.
**Guitarist:** Great rhythm feel, tasty soloist, able to play different styles, reader, quick study, sympathetic accompanist, etc.
**Keyboardist:** Reader, able to play different styles, good ear, comfortable on variety of keyboards, sympathetic accompanist, etc.
**Horn/String Instrumentalist:** Reader, able to play different styles, good ear, appropriate solo styles, doesn't overplay, quick study, etc.
**Singer:** Excellent pitch, range, vocal quality, able to sing different styles, lyric-writing skills, team player, etc.

Some of these attributes overlap, and some musicians must be evaluated in more than one category. You may have ideas not included above, and some might not apply to your situation. Example: If you are playing covers you probably don't care if a vocalist candidate can write lyrics.

Once you have made a list of the characteristics you need, prioritize them from 1 to 10, or however many skills you come up with. You can then rank auditioners on a predictive index, just like many businesses use to hire new employees. Make sure you have this list written down and agreed upon before talking with anyone about the opening. It will make the next steps that much easier.

■ ■ ■

### Fielding first phone calls

Your first contact with a potential band mate is almost always a phone call. The info gleaned from such a call can go a long way toward helping you decide who actually gets an audition. However, getting good info depends on asking the right questions.

Remember the important questions from the last chapter: Ask about experience. Transportation. Gear. Asking what kind of music someone listens to can be enlightening. If this is to be a soul/R&B band and the guitarist looking to audition says he listens to Sevendust, Metallica, and Mudvayne you can probably cross him or her off the list.

Some band leaders will even throw in a totally non-music question—we call this a "Bozo filter." Say your question deals with what a candidate like to do when he or she is not playing. It is a pretty safe bet that the guy who answers that he spends his non-playing hours hanging out in front of the local mall smoking cigarettes is not the kind of guy you want in the band. Bozo filters are totally optional but can be real useful.

One thing we have found useful is to make up a standard interview form, keep it next to the phone, and fill one out for each caller. This way you don't neglect to ask all the pertinent questions of each candidate. It also gives you something to refer to on the day of the audition, which can help you stay on track and organized.

Finally, for each candidate you decide to audition, provide an audition list of three or four tunes along with the keys and any other pertinent info. This is especially important for bands that play classic repertoire. For instance, if you are planning to do "The Letter", make sure to clue everyone in on whether it is the Box Tops original or the Joe Cocker remake.

## When they get there

First, you want to make sure to schedule things so that you have enough time with each candidate and so that overlap is minimal. Ideally, one player should be packing up as the next is arriving. Having everyone get there at the same time can be stressful and may leave you knowing less than you need to about each possible band mate.

Before you start playing, let the auditioner know if there is anything he or she needs to know about the tune. Did you add a solo section? Is there some other part of your arrangement that isn't part of the original version?

Run through the song once and, if there seems to be something worthwhile there, go back and try it again and see if it tightens up at all. Of course, let the new guy know if there is anything you need done differently.

After you've run all of the tunes, thank the player for coming out and let him or her know when you plan to make a decision. This is also the time to ask them if they have any questions you have not yet answered. It is *not* the time to get into philosophical discussions or to offer anyone the gig. Remember, there are more folks on the way.

## Before the final decision

The auditioning process can go on for weeks or months, but sooner or later you will make a decision. Before doing so, you'll want to spend a little more time on the phone with the final candidates. You'll want to make sure the new player is on the same page as the rest of the band. The best way to avoid a breakup a year from now is to avoid choosing the wrong player in the first place.

David Robinson, bassist/manager for the band Nailing Gello, emphasizes that it's more than just the music: "I have been in too many situations where each member of the group had his or her own idea of what the band should be aiming for. Some want to gig casually, while at the same time others need the cash and want to gig all the time. Some don't mind putting out a few bucks for roadies, and others mind it very much. Some want to play every gig possible ... weddings, clubs, parties, anything. Others will want to be more selective. The point is that a band should be just that—a band. People 'banded' together for a common purpose. If they don't agree on that purpose there will be tension. If they don't even get along in the first place there will be disaster."

Additional time on the phone, or club hopping with candidates will help ensure you make the best possible decision. When you do make the decision, be sure and have the courtesy to call losing candidates as well as the winner. You don't have to go into detail. Just be simple and quick: "I'm calling about your audition for our band. We appreciate you're coming out, but we've decided on another player. We really appreciate your time." If you're too chicken to call, then send a postcard. We can recall on several occasions giving the second-place candidate a call several weeks after hiring candidate #1 because the player we chose turned out to be a flake and quit. Musicians live in a small world, and it always pays to be courteous and professional.

## Band member personalities

Here's one more bit of non-musical advice: As you set off on this musical journey of starting a band, an understanding of a few of the typical musician personality types will be very beneficial. Being in a band is like a marriage—except you've got four or five people, not just two.

It's not necessarily a matter of one personality type being better than another. It's more about creating balance between the various personality types, and not having too many of one type in the band. You need a combination of all or some of these to be successful. Following are five musician personality types we've identified. They aren't meant to be black and white definitions, but they should give you a rough idea of what you will be dealing with when you put together a group of musicians. Understand as well that there is a bit of each of these in all of us.

**The Leader.** If you're the one starting a band, then in all likelihood you are the Leader type. You're organized, like to get things done. You're a little more left-brained than your typical musician. In fact, that's one of the faults of the Leader type: You're a little too intense and linear for most musicians. You tend to worry about everything. If you've had a great gig one night, on the way home you're already worrying about how the next gig will go, or what new songs you have to add to your set list to keep current.

**The Follower.** These are the types that tend to get along with everyone; they don't like to fight or stir up a problem. They are very dependable and fun to be around. Every band needs at least one Follower.

**The Struggling Artist.** This is the type who stands up for artistic integrity. This is the one who is writing originals (good or bad) and continually wants to work them into your set list, and eventually gives up playing covers altogether. Their whole life revolves around being a musician and "getting signed."

**The Selfish Player.** In most instances this type is very concerned about his or her individual progress as opposed to the group's. They assume that everyone comes to your shows to hear *them* play. Thus, they like their instrument to be loud, and they are always asking that they be turned up in the monitors. They like to jam and do solos as well. They set their gear up first at a gig and expect the PA system to magically set up by itself. In many cases, these types are truly very talented.

**The Groupie Magnet.** Doesn't matter what gender, male or female—this is the "looker" of the band. People come to your gigs just to appreciate their looks or magnetism. And the groupie magnet knows it. While they are at times excellent musicians, in most instances they are just average players; they get the job done.

# PREPARING FOR YOUR FIRST GIGS

*The whole objective of the first gig is to get the second gig.*
Jack Manzella
Midwest Talent Associates

So you've got the right players together—you found them or they found you—but you've still got to get a *band* together. Now the fun really begins. This chapter is designed to take you from your first band rehearsals to the day of your first gig, musically and organizationally: everything from choosing songs to running efficient rehearsals to putting together a set list. (What we don't include are the more technical issues, like your PA system and sound check. We've saved that for the final Tech section of the book.)

Regular and consistent rehearsals are a must for a starting band. If you're not concerned about gigging in the very near future, then you might get away with casually rehearsing once or twice a week to build your set list for a three-to-four-hour gig. Depending on the level of musicianship among the players, this may take months and months. This is because it's not just a matter of "learning" the songs together, but of playing them together enough so that you become tight as a band. The concept of being tight is all about the whole being greater than the sum of its individual parts. The old cliché of "Practice Makes Perfect" applies even more so to a group of musicians—that become a true band.

Because the first 40 or 50 songs your band learns will serve as the foundation of your entire set list for years to come, the extra time and attention put into learning these songs is a good investment for the future. When a gig is going south, there is no better way to win back your audience than by playing a tried and true standard that the audience loves—and the band knows inside and out and plays very tightly.

If you want to start gigging relatively soon, you'll want to consider rehearsing heavily for a month or so. By heavily we mean perhaps as many as five nights a week. These sessions don't have to be long, just a couple hours. (Balance this with the distance players are traveling to attend rehearsals.) Regular, consistent practices are more valuable and efficient than all-day or all-night practice sessions. Again, this is just for a short period of time—a month or so. This intense approach allows the band to grow tighter, more quickly. And then when you do play those first gigs, you will be more fully prepared than the typical upstart band. When that first month is over (or when you've started gigging), you can pull back to once or twice a week.

Quint was in a Top 40 cover band that had played together for so long, and was gigging so often, that they eventually stopped rehearsing altogether. For new songs, each player was responsible for *practicing* his or her part on his own, and then the band *rehearsed* those new songs during sound checks before each gig. But this same band, several years earlier, had rehearsed five to six nights a week to get ready for their first gig. The time they'd put in at the beginning made it easier for them to stay together for the long haul—and easier as well for new members like Quint to come onboard.

> *Learning your part is called "practice." Learning to fit all the parts together is called "rehearsal." Don't practice at rehearsal. At rehearsal, if you don't know your part and everyone else knows their parts, then you're not a band member, you're a problem.*
>
> Kevin Johnsrude
> The Nettles

## How to rehearse

Whatever the frequency, rehearsals should be prepared for and run in an efficient, professional manner. Rehearsal is not a learning session and it is not a jam session either. It's not at all a bad idea to have an agenda (in writing) and get it to the band in advance so everyone can prepare.

The following rehearsal scenario is simply a suggestion, designed specifically for starting bands.

**Setup and tuning.** This is not considered part of rehearsal. When you set up a rehearsal time, that means the band starts playing *at that time*. Eight p.m. means you are counting off the first song at 8. The reason for this is that if rehearsal "starts" at 8 and that is when everyone arrives, then actual playing won't begin until 8:30 or later. In addition to being a time suck, this can cause some real tension. If everyone arrives at 8 but it takes one band member five minutes to set up and another 25 minutes, then the one who was finished early sits and stews for 20 minutes. Not a good way to get started. It is far better for people to arrive with enough time to be set up, tuned, and ready at rehearsal time. Yes, it will mean some people have to get there earlier. (Hey, you wanted to be a drummer. Don't bitch that it takes time to set up your kit.) The best way to keep everyone on schedule is to make sure your written agenda includes *both* start time *and* setup time, as in "Rehearsal begins at 8; the room is available for setting up at 7."

**Warmup song(s).** Here you should play a song or two that you are very tight on and feel good about. The point here is to get a basic sound check and also to create a positive, confident feeling.

**Weak or older songs.** After each gig, you should note especially good and bad performances. In this part of practice, you should work on songs from your current set list that aren't quite together or are slipping. It is not necessary to play the entire song. It may be just an intro, a chorus, or a bridge that needs work. Or it may be just the vocals. For starting bands, this is the time to review earlier songs you have learned as a band but are starting to forget.

**New song(s).** This is where too many rehearsals start to break down, and it is almost always because someone is unprepared. Ideally, everyone will arrive *knowing* their parts, having spent the time listening and learning the songs on the CD that was passed out at a previous practice. If not, it is often better to just move on to something else than to spend time trying to nurse someone through his or her part.

The best approach to learning a new song as a band is to just barrel through the whole thing, ignoring mistakes and problems the first time out. It would be wonderful if that first pass resulted in a great performance, but it really almost never happens that way. After running through the song once, stop and talk about it. Where were the problems? First you'll deal with big, obvious things. The guitar player is playing the wrong chord on the chorus, or someone went to the bridge too soon. Things like that.

Smooth out the big problems and play through it again. Other less obvious problems will still be there—bass and keyboard parts are clashing, or the drummer is hitting an accent on the downbeat instead of the upbeat. Whatever. As you continue playing through and discussing, you'll eventually get it.

**Warm-down.** Just as runners "cool down" at the end of their workout, it is a good idea to "warm-down" a rehearsal. This is especially true when the rehearsal was a tough one where things were not going well. Always try to pick a fun song that everyone likes to play as your closer. It ends things on an up note and helps keep everyone enthused about playing. If there is time, this is when you can jam with extended solos, etc.

**Breakdown**. At the end of every rehearsal, the specific goals and songs that will be worked on at the next rehearsal session should be outlined. Again, individual players *must* learn their parts by that next practice. It is unfair and unprofessional for a player to show up at rehearsal unprepared.

**Vocal rehearsal and sectionals.** Unless you are very lucky, not everyone in the band will sing and, just like no one wants to stand around while the guitar player tries to figure out his part, the instrument-only players don't want to sit around doing nothing while the singers work out harmonies. That is why it is a good idea to have an occasional vocal-only session with just the singers in the band and a guitar or piano.

If you are in a large band, say one with a horn section, this approach can also work well. Bill has been playing in horn bands since the late '70s and has found that it is often better to learn new stuff in separate rhythm section (guitar, bass, drums, keys) and horn section rehearsals.

### Where to rehearse

There are lots of commercial recording and rehearsal spaces out there. But with studio time running up to $20-plus an hour, not to mention the hassle of loading in and out for every session, most musicians opt for homegrown solutions. We'll go over soundproofing, rehearsal gear, and recording rehearsals in the Tech section of the book, but here are a couple of basics to consider for now.

First, *try to rehearse in the same location every time.* This makes rehearsal seem a bit more serious, like you are going to work. (This, BTW, is a good thing.) Also, a consistent rehearsal space may mean you can leave some of the gear set up between sessions, allowing for more actual playing time at a rehearsal.

Second, *size matters.* An acoustic trio in a 6' x6' room may work, but put a five-piece band in the same space and you are asking for trouble. More people in less space almost always leads to some kind of a blowup. Most rehearsal spaces (garages, for example) are not air conditioned or heated and can get a bit uncomfortable. Add that to crowding and inevitable personell clashes and you have a potential big problem. Your rehearsal space need not be palatial, but make sure it is of adequate size.

Finally, *make the location central.* The further a band member has to travel for rehearsals, the more likely he or she is going to miss sessions or quit the band. This is also something to keep in mind when choosing players.

## Choosing songs

Before deciding *what* songs to learn, you need to know *how many* you need to learn. How many songs do you really need to know? This is a somewhat loaded question. Longtime bandleaders we interviewed in *Gig* magazine have said that 200 is a good starting number—but a reasonable and very doable number is probably closer to 40 or 50.

That may sound like a lot at first glance, but take a closer look. As a cover band, you will likely not be playing multi-band shows where each band does a 45-minute set and is done. Cover bands tend to play anywhere from three to five, 45-50 minute sets over the course of a night, and most bands will play 10-12 songs per set (note that this assumes that the band moves quickly between tunes). Do the math—10 songs per set for five sets is 50 tunes, four sets of 12 calls for 48 tunes. This makes 40 or 50 the *minimum* number of songs needed for your list.

How do you go about learning that much material?

Like anything else, you need a plan. If you are prepared and organized, it is no problem to learn three or four new songs in a three-hour rehearsal. You can learn even more if the individual players are extremely prepared. If not, plan on one song per rehearsal and staying in the garage for a long time.

The other dilemma is that, while you can learn three songs in a rehearsal, that does not mean you can have 30 songs ready in 10 rehearsals. This is because by the time you get to rehearsal number 10 and are learning songs 27-30, the band has forgotten several of songs 1-15. The best method seems to be to balance rehearsal time between reviewing stuff you are supposed to already know and learning new tunes. Some songs seem to stay tight without a lot of rehearsing, while others get loose real fast. As mentioned earlier, stay on top of your set list by regularly rotating older songs into your rehearsals.

Now, about choosing songs. This can cause serious problems if you have not done some of the other things we have written about in previous chapters, like making sure everyone is on the same page musically as far as band direction goes. (A bass player Bill once worked with actually started a fistfight over whether or not to play a certain song. No joke.)

Even in a Top 40 band, where the songs you play depend largely on what's on the *Billboard* charts, there are tricks to picking the right songs. Corky Hessler, a drummer and bandleader who has been gigging for more years than most of us have been breathing, lets us in on one of his secrets for picking tunes:

"As far as choosing songs to perform, I'll give away a secret that has kept me playing since 1961. I listen carefully to commercials on television. The producers of the commercials spend literally millions of dollars identifying the demographic they want to appeal to, and determining the Q (audience recognition for a song or name) before they make a commercial. I try to decide if the audience they are trying to entice is my audience, and if so, we work up that song. We play many of the songs currently being used in commercials. Another trick is to keep track of how many songs you perform that are on the various VH1 Top 100 songs lists. Listen to the radio station in your market that plays the kind of music your band learns, and check with the station to see if they have ever done a listener survey to compile a top 100 of that genre. Hopefully you know more than a third of the list. There are a lot of great songs out there that die a lingering death when played by a local band, simply because no one in the audience is familiar with them."

As far as who makes the decision on song selection, there are a couple of ways to go. Some bands with very strong leaders leave all of those decisions to the person in charge. This looks easy on the surface but often leads to problems because other band members might feel that they are not able to contribute. For most bands, it is important that everyone in the band be able to have a say in what songs you will learn.

Having said that, voting on individual songs is a nightmare that many times leads to dissension. One alternate method Bill has found to work well is to let everyone pick a song in a kind of rotation. He keeps a rotation list of band members (it could be organized by seniority, alphabetically, by height, or any way you like), and every time it's time to pick a new song, the person at the top of the list brings in three suggestions. He gets everyone's input and then he decides which of the three the band will do. Everyone gets a voice and they avoid a lot of fights.

### Creating a set list

*Think of it as a whole: how songs fit together in tempo, feel, key, rhythm, and lyrical content. In other words, don't play all your "I hate you" three-chord songs in G back to back. Don't hold your best song for an encore either—you may not get one!*
Tom Skidmore

While there will be some nuances from genre to genre, at most gigs you need to create a written document that tells everyone in the band what songs you will play and in what order. You'll have this taped to the floor, or at the front of your fake book, or maybe in large cue-card form toward the side of the stage. But putting a set list together is not just a matter of random choice and luck. When used correctly, your set list can be the difference between a mediocre gig and a great one.

"Once I finally learned how to put together a set list, the band really started controlling and playing the crowd. It really made a big difference in how the dance or gig went," says lead guitarist Rich Clark of the college-town group Up & Ups. While a set list may be the type of thing you always end up throwing together a few minutes before a show, putting a set list together long before you start gigging is not jumping the gun at all. Practicing songs in a certain order will prepare you to move directly from one song into another when performing. Following is a proven method of creating a set list that can really work for you and your band.

**Consult with band members.** First, whoever is writing the set list should consult with those players in the band who switch sounds or even instruments during the set. Guitarists and keyboard players switch sounds, but these days that usually involves just the press of a footswitch—no big deal. On the other hand, if a guitarist or horn player is physically switching instruments, that needs to be accounted for in your set order. (Bill couldn't understand why his band was taking so long between songs until he realized that because of the order in which he wrote the set, his sax player was switching between tenor, alto, and baritone saxes on almost every tune.) So, group several "like-instrument" songs in pairs so less time lapses between songs. Eliminate as much switching back and forth as possible without your sound becoming monotonous.

**Consult your vocalist.** Next, you'll want to ask your vocalist which songs are difficult to sing before his or her voice is really warmed up. Expecting your lead singer (or singers) to sound his or her best three songs into the gig is a little too much to ask. Save the hardest songs for the second and third sets.

**Lay out framework.** Your next step in the process is to pull out a piece of paper and number it in the following manner: 1-11, 1-11, and 1-13. This is the basic framework for a three-hour gig: two sets of 11 songs and one set of 13. (If it's a four-hour gig, it's 1-11,1-11,1-11,1-13.) Filling in the blanks is about as easy as doing a crossword puzzle—if you're good at crossword puzzles. (Another good way to do set lists is to maintain a song database on your computer.)

For most dances or club gigs, you need no more than six slow songs. Obvious exceptions to this rule are gigs such as proms, formals and wedding receptions. The reverse is true for wild parties, when you might play as few as three slow songs. But just to get started, throw slow songs in at numbers 4 and 8 in all three sets.

**Starts and stops.** The next step is to choose which songs you are going to end the gig with, as well as songs to end each set. Then, pick songs to begin each set with. Realize that at most dances (or clubs) the crowd is rather thin at the start. In many instances, people don't really start showing up until the beginning of the second set. This is why the songs you choose for the beginning of the second set are so important. They really set the mood for the rest of the night.

Save your best tunes for the last two sets and use set one as somewhat of a warmup set. If you're short a few tunes, play any songs you have to play twice right at the beginning, and chances are, no one will ever know. (Except club managers. Be careful about this because sometimes playing tunes twice really ticks them off.)

**Fill in the blanks.** The rest is about as easy as filling in the blanks on a crossword puzzle when it's three-quarters of the way finished. The key is to build momentum for a few songs and then throw the audience (or dancers) off and give them a bit of a rest with a slow tune. Too many fast tunes and you burn the crowd out; too many slow songs and you put them to sleep. If your group plays any songs that are difficult to dance to, you might want to put them in the first set. If you've got the audience going in the middle of the second set and you play an un-danceable or off-the-wall tune, the dance floor could clear and you might never get the crowd back.

And don't forget to vary the mood or vibe on your list. If you look at your set and see three consecutive uptempo rockers in the key of E, you can expect a bored audience by the mid point of that third tune.

## Going off the list

Even the best-made set list will sometimes not fit the gig, and you will find it necessary to go *off the list*—that is, to skip a song or substitute something in its place. This can happen because of an audience request, to keep a busy dance floor going even thought the list says the next song is supposed to be a ballad, or maybe to cover for a guitar player who broke a string or a singer who has to make an emergency bathroom trip. Every one of those scenarios (and more) will happen eventually if you gig long enough.

The challenge is to make the change smooth enough that few even realize a change has happened. It is also big reason why a single person needs to be in charge onstage.

This does not mean that no one else gets a say. It is totally acceptable for a band member to let the person in charge know that they think a change is called for. Just be discreet about it—announcing on mic between songs that "I hate the next song on the list, let's do something else" is bad form.

The best way to let the band know there is a change is some kind of prearranged hand signal, followed by a number or digits representing a song number. (Remember how we told you to number those set lists?) If appropriate to the gig, you might also do some on-mic patter that both sets up the tune for the audience and lets the band know what's up. But once the person in charge has decided to go off list, everyone else must go with the change without argument. If you don't like the change, talk about it on break or, even better, after the gig.

So, now you've gotten the band together, rehearsed, learned enough songs, and put together a set list. It's time to hit the stage and play your first gig. If you've prepared properly, all your hard work will soon start to pay off.

For more ideas on creating a set list and deciding on what new songs to learn, visit our web site at www.covergigs.com.

# SWEAT 5

# YOUR FIRST GIGS

*Getting ready for that first gig is one of the most fun things you can do as a performer.*

Corky Hessler

Even with a fully rehearsed set of great-sounding songs, there are marketing and promotional issues you'll have to deal with to get a gig in the first place. And once you book that gig, there are technology issues that can keep your fledgling band from pulling off a great first show. (We'll cover these Biz and Tech issues as the book progresses.) But for now, in this chapter, we want to step back and examine some of the issues you'll be facing on the day of your first gig, before you ever get onstage or play a single note. These may seem minor on the surface, but long-time giggers will tell you that they are the types of things that make or break new bands.

## A gig timetable

Getting organized on the day of a gig is sometimes a major stumbling block to pulling off a good show—and more important, having an enjoyable time. If you are rushed through setup and sound check, then you're not going to sound your best. Plus, you'll greatly reduce your chances of being asked back. The key to success lies in organization: laying down a schedule, complete with assignments and deadlines, and then sticking to it.

Doing a gig is like running a race—the hardest work comes in the preparation, and not necessarily in the actual race. In most cases, your actual playing time at a gig is somewhere between two and four hours. Yet you can put in as many as six to ten hours of work and travel (or even more) before the night is through. Loading, driving, setting up and sound-checking are just a few of the things you've got to put on your gig-night checklist.

The day of a gig, especially a one-night stand, should be planned with precision paralleling a military operation. A gig is a combination of so many different things; one seemingly insignificant problem can throw you off schedule, and there's nothing more embarrassing than starting late. As the old saying goes, "Plan your work, then work your plan."

Let's say your five-piece band has a club gig in town. Here's how you might plan that entire day from start to finish:

### 5 p.m.  Meet and load

If the band rehearses and the equipment is kept set up at a central location, then give yourselves at least an hour to break down and load the equipment into whatever vehicle (or vehicles) you'll be using. (If you're a duo or trio with a smaller PA, then plan on a half an hour.) Concentrate on getting everything loaded as fast as possible. It's easy to wander off into conversations about last night's date, the new Voodoo Glow Skulls album, etc., and fall behind schedule right from the start. And if you're not paying attention it's easy to forget stuff. Forgetting one simple cable can ruin your whole evening.

Some bands prefer to get in the habit of packing up after the last practice prior to a gig. Then, all that's left to do is load things into your vehicle and hit the road. If band members are traveling from different places, everyone should know exactly what time to arrive at the gig.

### 6 p.m.  Arrive & unload

As you pull up to wherever you are playing, send one player out to locate the booker or buyer as well as "the stage." (This is in quotes because in many cases you won't be playing on a stage at all.) While finding the stage isn't a problem at club gigs, we've spent as much as half an hour trying to locate who the heck's in charge and where exactly we're supposed to set up at some locations.

Here's a situation more than a few bands have been in: You show up to play a high school formal in the school's gym. The janitor lets you in, but there's no one else around so you start to set up on the north end of the gym. But sure enough, when you're about halfway done setting up, the school's dance director walks in and says, "No, no, that's all wrong. You're supposed to set up at the other end of the gym! Couldn't you tell that from the purple balloon bouquet's that we have set for you?" Have fun dragging all the equipment down to the other end.

Also, if it's a considerable distance between where you unload and where you'll set up, send someone else out to round up any extra dollies or moving carts (over and above your own). Unload all of the equipment before setting any of it up. Another problem that isn't so obvious is making sure there are plenty of electrical outlets where you'll be setting up. Sometimes it takes some creative thinking to get the electricity to where you need it.

If at all possible, try and leave your vehicle parked where you initially parked it to unload. This can save valuable time when the gig is over. If you move it, most times someone will park exactly where you unload. You will end up waiting until that person leaves or trying to locate the individual.

## 6:30 p.m. Set up

You know more about setting up your own equipment than anyone else, but here are a few pointers as far as the group goes.

Each player should have one or two other assignments besides setting up his or her own equipment. Quint used to have a guitarist in one of his early bands who would set up his amp and guitar and then sit around waiting for sound check. He would even go as far as plugging his amp's electrical cord into the outlet on the back of the bass player's amp and was not worrying about finding the venue's outlet. Quint finally had to make him understand that he was also responsible for setting up all the mics and running the snake back to the board. Then, and only then, he could set up his stuff.

The bottom line here is that if the same player does the same work each gig, he or she will become very quick at it; your set-up time will decrease from gig to gig until it's down to a minimum. Plus, work is spread out fairly among the band members. And expect some help from the drummer, too. Today's kits are more portable and can be set up more quickly, so drummers should have some sort of extra band assignment as well. (More on this in the Tech section.)

## 8 p.m. Sound check

While this chapter isn't about how to do a proper sound check, this is the time to consider some other things that revolve around it. For instance, some school and church functions require your sound levels to be checked with a decibel meter. The sound check is the best time to get this taken care of. Even without a decibel meter in a club, it's a good idea to assess your volume and general sound with the person who'll be handing over your pay at the end of the evening. Call it good PR.

Now is the time to also get the lighting levels set. This not only includes your stage lights (if you have any), but the lighting in the gym, auditorium, etc., if you're not in a club. Quint once played a church dance where the person in charge spent about 20 minutes (this is no exaggeration) adjusting the lights in the gym. He was worried it would be too dark, then he was worried it would be too light. There was no master dimmer control, so he went back and forth trying out various combinations of light switches.

Now, if there is any extra time after you've sound-checked and adjusted the lights, you can relax.

## 8:50 p.m. Get dressed and onstage

Give yourselves some time to throw on your gig clothes, check your hair, head to the bathroom, and then tune up a final time. Feel and look confident; you've done a lot of preparing for this gig, whether it's your first or one-hundredth. One word of caution: Don't stand up onstage for an extended time before you start, fiddling around with your instruments, practicing licks and riffs. This causes a lot of unneeded noise, and is irritating and unprofessional. Keep as quiet as possible until the first song begins.

## 9 p.m. The gig begins

In most cases, there aren't many people at a dance or club right when you're supposed to start. Even so, make it a point to start on time. It's another sign of your professionalism. Besides, why not get in a little practice?

Although the order of songs was discussed in the previous chapter, start out with songs with which you are most comfortable—not necessarily your most killer material, but the ones you know best and still enjoy playing. Some players may think that, since no one is there at the beginning of the night, it's a great time to get your weak songs out of the way. The problem with this is that you usually end up psyching yourselves out for the entire gig; you end up making more mistakes than normal. By starting a gig with songs you play well and know you sound great on, the momentum begins to roll and you'll play well the rest of the night. You'll find the songs you thought you'd be making slight errors in will come off sounding hot because you have confidence.

Stage presence is worth a quick mention here, even though there's a section on it later in this chapter. Your band's stage presence is not something any article can teach you. You must learn and develop it through trial and error. The key is to feel comfortable with being in the spotlight. Be yourself. Don't be someone you're not, or you'll end up looking like a lounge lizard. Spend as little time as possible between songs. People are there to dance or listen to music, not to hear musicians talk to each other or tune between songs. Sure, tell a few jokes or one-liners now and then. But keep in mind that you're a musician, not a comedian.

It is inevitable that some levels will have to be adjusted (monitors, stage levels, etc.). Remain calm and cool, and talk to your soundperson in between songs for the first couple of tunes. Just act like it's no big deal.

### 9:45 p.m. The first set ends

Man, that went fast. Here it is, the end of the first set already! The break is a time for the band to rest up a little for the next set and take care of things like a trip to the bathroom. You can also discuss any continuing problems with your soundperson. Relax and make yourselves available to the audience. Mingle, but don't make it seem like you're looking for a pat on the back. Talk to people, take requests, etc.

All band members should be back onstage tuning up, etc. a few minutes before it's time to start playing again. Make sure everyone in the band doesn't stray far from the stage; it's not too impressive when you're all ready to play and you realize your drummer is out in the parking lot having a cigarette. Quint remembers one awesome gig where the lead guitarist launched into the intro for an encore. But at about four bars in, everyone realized the drummer was nowhere to be found. Oops!

## 10 p.m. Second set begins

The second set is generally when a dance or club gig really starts to move. This is when you really have to capture the dancers and put the audience under your control.

## 11 p.m. Third set begins

If you've done your job right, the third set is nothing but a blast and is where the real payoff comes. On the other hand, if things haven't gone well, the third set will seem to last forever. But don't be surprised, when things have gone well, that you get called back for an encore.

## Midnight The gig is over

Unless of course this is a four-hour gig and you have one more set to play. You've had your fun, now it's time to get down to business again. Everyone in the band should begin working at the same time. Otherwise, resentment can build and tempers might flare if one player is still hanging out and talking to friends and groupies. Depending on how much equipment you have, it will take anywhere from 30 minutes to an hour and a half to break down and load the vehicle(s).

At any rate, break down your gear as quickly as you can and leave as soon as your job is finished. Nobody wants to wait around for the band to load up at 3 a.m.

## 1 a.m. Head for home

The gig was in town, so your drive back to the practice room or home will be just a few minutes. If you've got to unload tonight (this morning), then add another 15 to 30 minutes to your schedule. The equipment that weighed 50 pounds at 5 p.m. will now seem to weigh 250 pounds. Unloading takes longer than loading for this very reason.

You're probably exhausted by now, just reading this. So we won't say much more, just let you go home and sleep!

## What can slow you down

Even this detailed overview of the gigging process makes it all look too easy. A million things can slow you down and ruin the gig. Here are a few of them, in chronological order:

**Tardiness.** Just one or two players showing up late can throw you 20 or 30 minutes behind schedule. Band members constantly arriving late should not and cannot be tolerated. It's unprofessional and it's not fair to everyone else in the band. To avoid confusion, be sure to have everyone's cell phone number handy.

**Arguing.** People showing up late is just the type of thing that can set off an argument. But whatever the reason, make it a band rule never to argue on the way to, or at, a gig. It will slow you down, and you won't play well, either. And an audience can tell when band members aren't connecting onstage. Take care of any problems at the next band practice.

**Stopping to eat.** Okay, so it sounds ridiculous. But some people think "swinging by McDonald's for a Big Mac" takes no more than 30 seconds. In reality, it can take 10-20 minutes. It's also unfair to those who may have eaten before leaving. If you want to eat on your way to or from a gig, make it a part of the official band plan. A few years back, there was one player in Quint's band who always seemed to show up late for loading with a Big Mac and Coke in hand. His constant excuse was, "I had to get some dinner." It used to drive the rest of the band crazy, because it was like he was taking time out of his dinner schedule to help the band load.

**Long trips.** Traveling a long distance obviously takes more time than playing a local gig, but there are other things to consider besides the number of miles. First of all, if you're pulling a trailer, or you're in a large truck, then your average speed will probably be around 50 mph. So give yourself extra time. In addition, just deciding on how to get there can be confusing. Instead of relying solely on a map, you might ask whoever has hired you about the best route to take. Plan ahead when taking long trips and give yourselves plenty of time for gas and food stops. And if band members are traveling in different vehicles, be sure all have directions and contact phone numbers in case they get lost.

**Bad weather.** Rain and snow can put you way behind schedule, especially on long trips. It may be sunny in town, but an hour or two down the road it could be raining. Check out www.weather.com or call the highway patrol for weather conditions throughout your region.

Sometimes, weather problems can be avoided. During an April trek to Casper, Wyoming, it was reported that the roads were closed about two hours from our destination. But rather than let the weather reports win, Quint's band just decided to go for it. As it turned out, the road wasn't closed at all, and they got to the gig on time. What was so surprising was that there was hardly any snow at all on the highway that was supposedly closed. The point of this little story is don't believe everything you hear—even from the highway patrol.

**Vehicle breakdowns.** You can take great care of your vehicle, but you can never know when it is going to break down on the way to a gig. Sometimes the simplest things can create a nightmare. Here's a case in point:

A good friend of Bill's, along with the rest of his band, was on his way to a gig (40 miles away) in the band van. The gig was to start at 9 p.m., but the band didn't start playing until 11 p.m. What happened? Well, about halfway to the gig, the van broke down. A few of the band members hitched a ride and got a tow truck to come out, but the driver refused to tow the van 'cause it was too big. So the band ended up calling a few friends with pickup trucks to move the equipment into town. Believe it or not, the band got paid the amount stated in the contract, on the condition that a discount would be offered the next time the band played. By the way, the van cost less than $10 to fix.

**Lazy players.** Everyone has different work habits. So among several band members you are going to find hard workers, medium workers ... and bums! The key is to set an example and always work at a brisk pace. Work when it's time to work, play when it's time to play —and save the arguments over who needs to work harder for the next band meeting

**No spares.** Broken strings, busted drum heads, and blown fuses are just a few of the breakdowns that can happen during a gig (or just before). Who needs the high pressure of driving around an unknown neighborhood at 7:45 p.m. looking for a Radio Shack so you can replace a blown fuse? A good gig kit should contain backup accessories for sound reinforcement gear as well as individual players. (More on this in the Tech section of the book.)

First gigs are always a challenge. To meet that challenge head-on, learn as much as possible about the gig in advance. Prepare for the worst. Expect the best.

## Stage presence

Thus far, we've outlined some of the things that most beginning giggers never really think about but that can make all the difference between a good band and a great one (and the difference between good- and great-paying gigs). Besides playing tight and being organized, your band's stage presence will also set you apart from the competition. In an early issue of *Gig*, British writer Dave Howard wrote an article on stage presence that included a great story about a once-unknown performer.

■  ■  ■

I suppose we can all remember gigs where we were stunned by a performance. I remember one such, some ten or more years ago. (Okay, I confess, it was more than ten years, but how much more I won't say.) The event was a college Christmas party, imaginatively entitled the "Snow Ball." You can guess what it was like: dinner jackets, evening dresses, and an overwhelming smell of rum and black currant in the toilets. The college had no dedicated concert hall, so the refectory was pressed into action as the live music venue for the evening. The hall's usual capacity of 600 was eaten into by the presence of a fair-sized stage, but for the support acts at this highlight of the year, the reduced space was no problem. What was a problem was the lack of an audience.

Hardly anybody ever watched the support bands at these events. It was a question of priorities, you see. The adjacent bar was packed until late, but unfortunately drinks weren't allowed in the refectory. The bar would close prior to the headline band taking the stage, but until then, faced with the choice between a support band and booze, well, what was any self-respecting student supposed to do?

Being a musician I had a reason, if not a duty, to be curious about every band that visited the college, and at this particular Snow Ball I found myself with a handful of others watching a three-piece by the name of Barbed Choir. I remember standing transfixed, with a smile on my face. The drums and backline were draped in camouflage netting, and the band's appearance would likewise not have been out of place in a combat zone. What impressed me, though, was the singer/guitarist. For the duration of their 45-minute set, he entertained the five or six of us in that hall as if we were 10,000. He played the stage as if it were an instrument, and although we could have been embarrassed to applaud, dotted about as we were, he dared us to join him in the game, and we found ourselves whistling and cheering in response.

When I saw him next, in a small local venue, he was more fortunate. He still couldn't be said to be entertaining the masses—there may have been 30 or 40 people there—but my opinion was confirmed. He was a star! When the band finished the set, the stage was invaded by a horde of enthusiastic followers who proceeded to pack away his gear for him. Not paid roadies, you understand—just moths, caught in the starlight.

What those performances showed me was that stage presence isn't simply a function of fame. It is a weapon in the performer's artillery that should be employed at the earliest opportunity.

Of course, for some (mentioning no names, of course), conveying a sense of stage presence has become a matter of spending a sum equivalent to a small nation's gross national product on enough technology to launch a spy satellite, and then making it all flash like some over-specified Christmas tree. But I remember Bono (oops, I mentioned a name!) on that same wobbly college stage, and there was no denying it—he had a compulsive, irresistible stage presence.

For the real stars of this world, stage presence is an essential part of performance. The late Michael Hutchence of INXS once said, "When you walk up those steps to the stage it feels like sparks are flying through you. I get tears in my eyes—I know this sounds really schmaltzy—but I just want to give." The megastars are those who are not only born with stage presence and have a certain charisma, but also have a genuine need to express it.

That doesn't mean that the rest of us are doomed. It's just that we have to work a bit harder. Stage presence can be cultivated, and even those who are born with it often need to refine it. One notable British all-girl soul band was signed to a major label for a year before releasing anything; they spent the time being groomed, learning how to behave in interviews, taking dancing lessons, and learning how to communicate with a mic stand. So what do you do if you want to develop your own sense of stage presence?

The biggest step you can take is to build trust between you and your fellow performers. Forget about being cool. Forget about maintaining a superior image. What works far better is building an atmosphere in which no one is scared of looking completely stupid, and in which you know that your fellow performers will support you when you fall.

Actors and other performing artists have this built into their training, where it is recognized that mutual trust is an essential part of a good performing group, and musicians can do a lot worse than attend some acting classes. Even better, try dance lessons, as I once did along with the five other members of my then-band. What an ungainly sight we must have made. Again, good lessons will incorporate trust exercises, but at the very least, once you've all seen each other fall over whilst trying some new movement, you won't worry about tripping over guitar cables as you run about the stage.

Go to the books website to discuss stage presence on our message boards. www.covergigs.com

■ ■ ■

## Odds and ends

We'll finish off this chapter with a great set of tips from *Gig* writer Riley Wilson. These tips will also close out the Sweat section of the book. In the next section—which we call Biz—we'll look at all of the business and marketing aspects of being in a successful band. In many instances, mastering these skills is almost as important as mastering your instruments.

### Ten things that will keep you in the garage

**Your song list**: Aside from the rare situation where campiness or something equally risky is called for, "Tie a Yellow Ribbon," "Annie's Song," or anything by the Bay City Rollers spell instant doom. And if you're an alt rock band, try to be different. No, I know you're already different, I mean different from all the other alt rock bands in your neighborhood.

**Your look**. Nehru jackets are fun to remember but not to look at. This category also includes beads, square shades, and anything made of polyester.

**Your equipment**. Without mentioning any names—you know who you are—some people must definitely learn the term "state of the art." Drums re-done with wallpaper or foil, and homemade speaker cabinets that look like tomato crates, will assure a long career in the garage.

**Your drummer.** "Yankee Doodle Dandy" and other patriotic march-type beats have their place—the garage.

**Your vocals.** Wayne Newton, Tom Jones, and other Las Vegas-type vocalists—to the garage.

**Your promo kit.** Demos done on ghetto blasters sound best in the garage. Bios written in pencil on three-ring notebook paper make perfect welcome mats in the garage.

**Groupies.** "Money for nothing and your chicks for free"? Well, not exactly. Everything has its price. If you're going into this business just for the groupies, you won't get your equipment past the garage door—and you probably won't get any groupies either.

**Your hair.** Too long, too short, too many colors! Play it smart and be yourself.

**Your curfew.** I once played in a band with a guy who couldn't stay out past 10 p.m. Of course, no one in the band knew that until our first gig, when at 10 the bass player announced he was leaving. (He was already late!)

**Your band's name.** If your mother loves it, if you're not a little embarrassed to admit it to your rich Uncle Henry, or if your business cards could double for a carpet cleaning company, then you've got a lousy name.

*Section Two*

# Biz

# MARKETING YOUR BAND

*In our band, we all agree on one thing: Satisfaction comes from performance, but success comes from marketing.*

Dick Roark

In many ways marketing your band is like marketing any other small business. You need a name that reflects your product or service, an image that expresses the unique personality of that product, and an understanding of the geographic and marketing characteristics of the area in which you are competing. You need a complete understanding of the needs of your customers. In sum, you've got to set yourself above and apart from the competition.

This doesn't mean that the "artistic integrity" of your band will be compromised as you go through these steps, but you do have to realize that success depends highly on your ability to communicate the features and benefits of your product to your consumers. While all of us certainly appreciate the artistry of many major recording artists, keep in mind that *all we see* is the end product. We don't always see or realize the amount of promotion and marketing efforts that are behind these successes—or, if we have seen them, we aren't conscious of how much those efforts have actually affected us.

Just like any product or service targeted at consumers, it all starts with a name.

## Your band name

Due to the niche nature of marketing your band, the first question you need to ask yourself is whether your act's name matches the type of music and venues you hope to play. In fact, we believe that, because your band is playing cover material, its name is more important to its success than it would be with original acts. Several examples from our own and others experiences will illustrate what a difference a name can make.

A few years ago Quint started a duo that performed unplugged classic rock in coffeehouses and restaurants. In the beginning they called themselves "Randle and Blankenhorn," just using their own last names like a lot of duos do. And even though they got really good response at the few gigs they were getting, they just weren't playing as much as they wanted. Quint also didn't feel real comfortable announcing the name of the group during performances; those last names didn't exactly roll off his tongue. So after several months of wanting to improve their situation, Quint was looking at their set list and came to a realization: They were playing a lot of old Beatles and Eagles covers. He also remembered having used this to describe the group to friends: "We play a lot of old Beatles and Eagles, a lot of harmonies, that kind of stuff."

After some thought he and his partner literally put two and two together, changing the name of the group to The Beagles and adding a *subtitle* (a unique marketing phrase or selling proposition) to all their promotional material: "BEAtles, eaGLES and Other Classic Soft Rock." They even added a cheesy picture of a beagle to their logo. And people—bookers and listeners alike—got it! They went from just a couple of gigs a month to a nearly fully booked schedule. Shows became more fun as well. The name fit the members' personalities and the audiences they were playing to. This was not due to any big change in what the group was playing, but a change in how they perceived themselves and how they presented themselves to their audiences. (Think back to our discussion of stage presence in the Sweat section.) They set themselves apart from and above the competition. (They also became a trio, and even though Quint moved from the area, the group continues successfully as of this writing.)

The wrong name can kill a group as well. In the mid-'70s a band came on the scene called The Babys. This group, unlike most "The" groups of the 1980s, was not playing '60s-influenced, Phil Spector–style rock & roll, but music similar to Bad Company. The lead vocalist was John Waite (who eventually hit No. 1 with the song "Missing You" and also played with the band Bad English later in his career). Keyboardist Jonathan Cain, who was in The Baby's before he joined the mega-successful Journey, said in an interview with Robert Hilburn of the *L.A. Times* that the name "The Babys" followed them like a curse and eventually led to the demise of the band. The Go-Go's could probably have gotten away with a name like The Babys, but The Babys couldn't.

However you come up with a name, make sure it is something you can live with over the long haul. Bill has been performing under the name "Rev. Bill and the Soul Believers" for almost 20 years. It came about in a weird way. Bill and some friends started jamming in college, and someone came up with the name Billy Anonymous and the Psychopathic Killers. When the jam became a band they used that name at first. Problem was that they were playing classic R&B and soul covers, but every booker they approached was convinced they had to be a punk band. Bill went to meet with his co-band leader, Jake Kelly, to discuss it. When Bill arrived at the house, Jake introduced Bill to his dad saying, "Dad, this is Reverend Bill. He's my spiritual adviser."

The name stuck, and Bill has been *stuck with it* ever since. They started riffing on the "reverend" name and the kind of music they were playing, and the name of the band just kind of happened. They did have a few problems when bookers thought they were a church act, but after a while a unique image grew from there. They actually tried to drop the Rev. Bill part a few years ago and just use the Soul Believers, but promoters and bookers continued to refer to and advertise the band as "Rev. Bill", so they gave up even trying.

In creating a name, evaluate the names of the bands whose songs make up the majority of your set list, the types of songs you are playing, the demographics of your bookers and audience, and of course the personality of your group's members. Then make sure the name "matches" the type of music you are playing and the image you are trying to portray.

Quint judged a battle of the bands recently, and there were several examples of both good and bad names. The good band names were ones like Drop Out High (grunge) and the River Ranch Band (country). Both of these bands "sounded" like their names and looked the part as well. Before he even heard them perform Quint had a rough idea of what he was in for. But what about the band that called itself "Nice"? You couldn't tell by just the name that this was a very heavy-sounding rock band that was trying to create an ironic twist with their name. And then there was the band "$\pi$"—the mathematical symbol. Again, they were a very heavy rock band, but just imagine marketing this band over the phone and trying to explain that the name of your band was the symbol, not the kind of pie you eat. (The artist formerly known as The Artist Formerly Known As Prince tried this, and even he went back to his original moniker of Prince.)

So be sure your name matches both the material you are playing and the audiences to which you are marketing yourselves. This is more important for cover and show bands than it is for all-original bands, because with cover bands you are conveying a product, while with original bands you are in many cases creating a unique brand identity. Plus, you want to make it easy to communicate. When you've got just a few seconds to get the attention of a booker, you don't want to have to be explaining you are a symbol, not an actual pie. Your image will then flow directly from your name, your material, and your collective personalities.

## Image

Pop music has become 90 percent image oriented. So your image is especially crucial for bands that play cover material. Look at it this way: When mobile DJs started to really get into the market in the '80s, the days when being a good band was enough to get regular work came to an abrupt end. The DJ was one guy and could charge half of what bands were asking and make twice as much or more than the average band member for the same gig. Worse for many bands of the time, some of the DJs put them to shame when it came to image and performance skills. There are DJs who are master beat-makers who can seamlessly spin several hours of nonstop, beat-matched dance music. These guys are every bit as creative and just as much musicians as the hottest guitarist or sax player in town. But there are also DJs with no technical knowledge beyond running a couple of turntables (these days more likely a dual CD player) and a rudimentary PA, but who have an appealing image, charm, and charisma.

This is your competition.

When Bill was coming up in Top 40 bands, he was fortunate enough to hook up with an agent who insisted his bands look good, and a manager—okay, he was the rhythm guitarist's dad and he was only around about a month—who gave the band one piece of image advice he has never forgotten: "The band should never be mistaken for the audience."

It's great advice. Just as marketing is a way to set yourself apart from and above the competition, the way you look onstage sets you apart from the audience. It makes you different, special. But you've got to strike a balance. Sure, you don't want to look like your audience, but you don't want to look like a Las Vegas show band either—unless you are one. Just like your band name, your image should look and "feel" like the sound of the artists and bands whose material you are covering. It should also meet your audience's expectations of how your kind of a band should look. A lot of your image has to do with what you wear.

## Dress the part

Unfortunately, it's not as simple as just saying, "Dress nice." We have learned over the years that "nice" has too many possible interpretations. Some musicians will take it to mean it's okay to wear sweats as long as they don't have any visible holes. And sometimes "nice" is all wrong.

An example from the late '80s proves this point: Bill's band favored black slacks, white shirts, skinny ties, and red hi-top sneakers for club gigs. For higher-end private gigs, they ditched the sneakers and added black suit coats. This worked fine until a couple of wedding gigs where the band's two sax players were mistaken for waiters and asked to bring various items to various tables. Then there was the time Quint went outside for some fresh air during a break at a church-sponsored dance, then had a hard time getting back in because he didn't meet the required dress standards.

Part of the formula depends on your role in the band. If you are a backup player, take your cues from the leader, who will often specify what is to be worn. But if you are a singer or other front-person, you need to take some time and really think about how you want to present yourself.

It makes a difference. After years of ensuring that his band presented a unified and sharp image, Bill started to let things slide until one day he looked at the stage and realized that he was wearing shorts and a T-shirt, and that the entire band looked less than professional. He has since reformed and gone from sloppy to suits onstage. The result? The amount of money the band was able to charge for a typical gig nearly doubled

But as the quality of gigs went up, it was no longer enough to just wear a suit onstage. Lately, the nice black suit has been replaced with a couple of very brightly colored suits with "sweep" jackets that hang past the knee and a purple "pimp" hat—clothes that scream "he must be in the band."

Looking good is crucial, but be practical. Those sweep suits look cool, but they have to be dry-cleaned after every gig, which can get expensive. It's also important that you are comfortable enough to actually play, and play well. For example, drummers get a bit of slack in the dress department. This is because they are largely hidden behind the kit, and time and groove count more than fashion.

One last note on the subject of dress: Every gig matters. Barbara Myler is the president of Summit West Management in Southern California. She books a bunch of cool gigs with name acts, as well as the personal projects of sidemen to the stars. A couple of years ago she booked a guitarist whose regular gig was backing a superstar R&B performer known for being a dapper dresser. "He arrived wearing shorts and a T-shirt, but I didn't think anything of it. I assumed those were just his set-up clothes," she says. To her shock and dismay, this pro, who should have known better, took the stage and began performing in the same sloppy duds. "You know," Myler muses, "he was really quite good, but I never booked him again."

'Nuf said.

## Geographic market

Beyond looking inward, you need to look outward. This comes down to deciding how far you are willing to travel and at what cost. When Quint was in college the cover band he was in would drive up to eight hours (in the band-owned Chevy Blazer with a U-Haul trailer in tow) for well-paying Friday- and Saturday-night dances in—count 'em—five Western states. It was good fun and good money. But years later he was performing in a trio that was keeping busy almost every weekend on most gigs within a 20-minute radius of his home.

Take a map and draw a circle in your chosen radius from your home base. This will help you identify how far you are willing to travel and also help you locate smaller towns and venues that you might not have thought about otherwise. Also, consider how often you should play the same place. Expanding your geographic market means there will be less chance of burning out regulars at one or two local venues.

Musicians chasing the rock star dream may be willing to sleep in a van and live on beef jerky for the honor of being "on tour" ... for a while. But eventually the van life gets old, and most players who have been at it a while and who are trying to make a living expect out-of-town gigs to pay significantly better than local gigs.

Two examples from Bill's playing past come to mind. Back in the late '80s his band played pretty regularly at a club in Santa Barbara, two hours north of their home base near Los Angeles. The gigs paid only okay, but it was enough to cover meals and motel rooms, and Santa Barbara is a very cool little coastal college town, so the band treated the gigs as working vacation weekends.

Flip side. A couple of years ago, an agent offered his band a private party gig at a Vegas casino. On the surface it sounded pretty cool—Vegas is fun, the band would be playing for "high rollers," and one meal was included at the party itself. The gig also paid better than most local club gigs, though no better than a local private party, and no rooms were included in the deal. Plus it's a five-hour drive, and the pay would cover meals and maybe rooms but not any kind of extra—this in a town where you can drop $100 in just a couple of minutes if you're not careful. The band ended up turning down the gig.

So now that you know who you are, and you know your geographic target market, you've got to translate this into marketing materials.

## The promo kit

First off, let's be real clear about the difference between customers and fans. When your musical endeavors are about being a recording artist and gigs are a way of introducing your original music to potential fans, then those fans who buy your recordings in effect "sign the check"—they are your customers. On the other hand, when you are playing cover material and providing entertainment in bars, clubs, and private gigs, the listeners are indirectly your customers, but they are first customers *of the venue*. Your true customer is the person who pays you, *i.e.*, the venue owner or event booker. While your listeners are at the various venues you'll be playing, you've got to get past the gatekeepers before you can reach them. These gatekeepers can range from a big fat bar manager (complete with a cigar in his mouth) to a seven-person committee made up of high school students. Your first weapon here is your promo or press kit. This is kind of like a résumé for the band and should include several things: business cards (with logo), a bio or band "story," a demo tape or CD, a song list, a photo, and any press clippings or reviews. Let's look at several of these items more closely.

## Your logo

Once you have decided on a name, you need to figure out how to present it graphically. The graphic representation of a company or band name is called a *logo*. Take into consideration the image you want to portray, how the logo will be used, and where it will be printed. Your logo should be easy to read, look professional, and feature a simple color combination. Some of the most effective logos have only one color.

Enlist a good graphic artist to design and produce your logo. How do you find the right one? Your best bet may be a local art student who is willing to work cheap for the experience. Another possibility is to look at other local bands and their logos. Find some you like and ask the bandleader about the artist. You may be surprised to find out that it is a member of the band. (Many artists moonlight as musicians and vice versa. Creativity is not always limited to a single outlet.)

Recently Quint was looking at a bulletin board at a music store. There was a extremely well-designed flyer soliciting a guitarist. The logo was totally professional. It turns out that one of the band members was a graphic artist by day and a musician by night. When Quint went to see the band live, the logo proved to be a heck of a lot better than the band itself. Even so, the logo did its job—it got Quint to check out the band.

Regardless of how you go about finding an artist, make sure you look at their prior work. Make sure that their artistic style is compatible with your musical style. Things like logos can go a long way in defining a band to potential fans. In sum, the logo should extend the name of the band into visual form.

Is someone else already using your name? Go to www.covergigs.com for links on how to do a trademark search.

## Business cards

As soon as you get a good logo, then get some business cards made up ASAP. You're not in a working band unless you've got a business card. A quick-print place will do, and places like Kinko's have special business card services. You can even fake it for a short time with business card paper kits and software for your Mac or PC. In addition to the obvious stuff like names and phone numbers, include a unique selling proposition (subtitle); this further defines your niche. For example, as mentioned earlier in Quint's story about the Beagles, their unique selling proposition was "BEAtles, eaGLES and Other Classic Soft Rock."

## The demo tape or CD

This is your real calling card—the thing that will truly represent you to potential clients. It is of major importance.

You can spend anywhere from $5 to $5,000 for a quality demo. While the method and cost is definitely something to consider, your goal should be to capture "your sound" on tape. If this can be done with a direct line from your mixing console into a two-track DAT recorder during a live performance, then that's one route you could take. On the other hand, if the gigs you are booking require a tape with better audio quality, then you might want to take advantage of multitrack recording. But don't let the money required for multi-tracking scare you. A cover band demo is very different from a demo of an originals band trying to land a recording contract. It's a lot simpler and much less expensive.

There are basically three options available, each with its advantages and disadvantages. At the lower end of the price scale is using a DAT or cassette and a few mics to record direct to two-track. Your second option is to use one of the many multitrack digital recorders on the market today. You can buy one for about the same amount it would take to go into a decent studio and complete a full-blown demo.

The third and most expensive option would be to go into a multi-track studio and go for the gusto.

We won't deal with the technicalities of recording here (see the Tech section for some tips), but we will point out a few other important factors to consider when putting together a cover band demo tape.

Unlike an originals band demo, the songs you'll present on this demo are already produced and arranged. So it takes much less time to prepare and cut a cover demo than one for original music. This is important if you're considering going into a multitrack studio that charges by the hour.

In preparing for your recording session, choose seven or eight songs. Chances are you might only record five of them, but you'll want to prepare more so you can choose the tunes that end up sounding the best. Most recording artists use this technique when cutting album tracks.

Recording five songs for a demo tape may sound like a lot of work, but you won't be recording entire songs. You should record segments of these songs, lasting a minute to a minute-and-a-half each. This way, your demo ends up lasting five to seven minutes instead of 18. Listeners will get bored wading through entire songs. Remember, they've heard them before; they've just never heard *you* before.

In addition to simplifying things for the listener, recording short segments—an intro, verse, and chorus, for instance—makes your job much easier. You can pick and choose parts of songs that you perform best. Exploit your strong points and cover your weaknesses. If your guitarist doesn't play a particular lead too well, but your vocalist nails her part on the same song, forget the guitar solo. In other words, arrange the song to fit your needs. Fade in, fade out, come in abruptly—whatever. The important part is the performance.

When choosing songs, stick to classics and standards. Stay away from gimmick songs and what will likely be one-hit-wonders. You don't want a song that's been dropped from your list still haunting your demo tape a few months after recording it. Listeners might say, "These guys are pretty behind the times. What a silly song. Do you really want to hire this band?" Play it safe and record sure-fire, long-term hits. If you are in a hard-core Top 40 band, you will need to show that you are current, but this is easily done by including a couple of recent tunes that have spent a lot of time on the charts on a printed song list that is updated for each potential client.

Also, vary the tempo and feel of the songs—record three fast songs and two slow songs. While this may not be a true representation of your fast songs/slow songs ratio, it lets listeners know that you aren't overly rowdy and can play a wide variety of gigs. It really all depends on the type of gigs you want to be playing. The order of the songs might be something like fast, slow, fast, fast, slow. Again, your song list will give clients an idea of your overall balance. Also, consider putting your strongest material first, in case the booker doesn't take the time to listen to the whole demo. You can encourage him or her to play more of it by attaching a label that includes titles, tempos, and lengths for each item. Remember how we said earlier to record more than the five songs that will end up on your tape? Well, there's another reason for that: Different kinds of gigs call for different kinds of tapes. If your band does both clubs and casuals, you will need a tape for each. Some songs will work on both kinds of tapes, but a club tape should generally be more uptempo, and a casuals tape should include at least one pop standard ("Misty," "All of Me," etc.).

If your band decides to go into a real recording studio, here's some more advice: Don't catch "multitrack fever" and do an excessive amount of overdubbing. Keep overdubs to a minimum: the rhythm track, the vocals, the solos—that's it. If you can't pull it off live, then it shouldn't be on your demo. The main reason to paying for a recording studio should be for the high audio quality of the finished demo, not the chance to do a million overdubs. On the other hand, if you end up recording the demo on your own gear, then there won't be much room to overdub, if any at all. And you'll probably end up being your own engineer.

A couple of other important issues:

**CDs, not tapes.** CD burners are common enough now that there is no reason for your demo to be on tape (even though we use the old terminology above). These days, CDs are expected.

**Licensing.** The brouhaha over Napster and file sharing triggered some legal changes that can have a major effect on cover bands. CD duplicators must require any client to provide proof that they either own the material on the CD to be dubbed or have paid to license it. For this reason alone it is best to just dub your CDs yourself. As long as you are not selling your demo, you should have no problems with licensing, but *you will not be able to take it to an outside service for duplication.* This is why you won't be able to post these types of demos on Internet sites such as MP3.com.

## Band photo and bio

Let's start with the photo. It needs to visually communicate what kind of band you are. The easiest way to do this is to have the band members dress as though they were on a gig and hold instruments. An interesting background can help your photo stand out from others, but just make sure the background does not overwhelm the band.

The photo needs to be well composed, well lit, and pro-looking. It needs to be polished and of high enough quality that it can be easily reproduced. If you have to choose, B&W is better than color, but it is nice to have both. Once the photo is shot and processed, you will need to have copies made in 8x10 format with your name and contact info at the bottom. (Though we're seeing more photos without contact info, probably because items such as area codes change so frequently.) On the next page there's an example of the kind of photo we're talking about.

There are so many quality automatic cameras out there that you can probably do this without hiring a photographer. As long as you have a friend or family member or even band member with a good eye who can set things up, anyone can push the shutter button and take the photo. (For his band's latest promo shots, Bill had his wife—who is a designer and artist—set everything up and compose the shots. But because she sings in the band, she had to be in the photo, too. And so their 11-year-old daughter shot the actual photos—which have been used for gigs ranging from local clubs to festivals that attract several thousand listeners.) If you do want to spend a little money for higher quality, then consider finding a student photographer, or contact the photo department at your local paper for a freelance photographer.

Bios need to be well written, short, and to the point. Avoid terms like "colossal talent", even if you are one—it comes off as cheesy and will turn most people off. If you are not much of a writer, consider shelling out a few bucks to a local reporter or even an intern at a PR agency and have the bio written by someone who knows how to do it. Just remember that an amateurish bio, photo, or demo will make potential clients think the band is amateurish as well.

In addition to clients, you will want to send this material to your local newspaper. Especially with club gigs, a mention in the paper can bring in more people, which will make it more likely that the band will get asked to return for another gig.

# Railroad Earth

Todd Sheaffer – vocals, guitars
Tim Carbone – violin, vocals
John Skehan – mandolin, piano
Carey Harmon – drums, percussion, vocals
Dave Von Dollen – bass, kalimba, vocals
Andy Goessling – guitars, dobro, banjo, marxophone,
flute, pennyswhistle, ukelele, clarinet, vox

Once upon a time, a bevy of rabid music fans descended upon a crowded, humid club, anxiously buzzing about an elusive band they'd heard only via the Internet. For weeks, people had been downloading and forwarding a handful of mp3 files, and reading gushing reviews from the few who had been lucky enough to see them perform live. You could feel the anticipation build as the crowd moved toward the stage, waiting for the music to begin. A few skeptics were among the crowd, as that much praise and adoration can raise suspicions. However, within seconds of the first frenzied, acoustic-driven notes, it became clear that the hype and passion for Railroad Earth was right on the mark.

This tale really begins at an informal bluegrass picking party at multi-instrumentalist Andy Goessling's rural western New Jersey home in January of 2001. Joining the musician extraordinaire on that fateful day is his bandmate from the notorious Blue Sparks from Hell, blazing violinist Tim Carbone. Mandolin player John Skehan arrives with his unique rhythmic style, adding a fierce counterpoint to the mix. And Carey Harmon lays down a solid, jazzy backbeat against the snaking upright bass of New School jazz major Dave Von Dollen. Rounding out the jam session is lead singer, songwriter and guitarist Todd Sheaffer, co-founder of the now defunct band, From Good Homes (RCA Records). The jam begins and suddenly there is a spark. They're on to something here - something that is worth investigating.

John Skehan    Andy Goessling    Tim Carbone    Todd Sheaffer    Dave Von Dollen    Carey Harmon

## Railroad Earth

Sugar Hill Records Media
120 31st Ave. N.
Nashville, TN 37203
(615) 297-6890

But once you've invested time and money in your valuable press kit, don't send it out recklessly. Do some research. If you're mailing it to your local music magazine or newspaper, double-check that you're addressing it to the right person—employee turnover rates in publishing are high. If the paper has a managing editor and an arts-and-entertainment editor, call and ask which one should receive your package; procedures vary. Also, talk to other musicians who've been covered there. Did the paper contact them after receiving their press kit, or did a music writer happen to catch one of their shows and then pitch a story about them to the paper? It's frequently the writers who champion bands and determine who gets covered.

Just as it pays to know the workings and business concerns of booking agencies and venues, it's wise to learn how your local publications operate. For instance, be aware that editors rarely have time to get out and hear live bands themselves because they're usually chained to their desks by 60-hour-per-week schedules; they depend on their writers to keep them informed. Find out which writers and photographers cover your scene—and network, network, network.

### Using the Web

Cover bands are not going to be uploading songs and promoting their music on the Web in the same way as original artists, but there are several things you can do to promote your band online. (You can't legally distribute your complete recordings of others' songs.) For example, your band bio and schedule should be uploaded. (Club owners love it when the bands they hire provide examples of how they are promoting their shows and drawing customers into the venues.) You should also collect email addresses as part of your mailing list.

Now, with these tools in hand, you're ready to start booking gigs.

## BIZ 2

# BOOKING YOUR BAND

*Many clubs, if you draw well, won't care if the band is a half dozen albino monkeys playing kazoos. They want business, and if you give them business they'll want you back. However, if you are kazoo-playing monkeys, your crowd won't return.*

Jack Manzella

You've got a name, players, a promo pack with demo, and a solid set of 30-40 tunes ready to perform. You're ready to start gigging—which is really where the hard part starts.

Yes, friends, it's time to start looking for work. While at some point you may start working with an agent who will take care of your bookings, in these early stages you will almost definitely have to book yourself. Or to put it more bluntly: Even with decent tape and promo package, you'll still being doing a lot of begging, cheating, and clawing for those fist few gigs.

This chapter is designed to make the non-musical transition from rehearsal studio to stage less painful and a lot more fun.

### Pros and cons of booking

Before we get into the process of self-booking, let's take a quick look at the pros and cons of this approach. Like we just said, in the beginning you will almost always have to book yourself. Booking agents work on a commission (usually 15 percent) and are generally only interested in working with bands that have already established themselves to a degree so the agent can actually make some money. That means bands need to be working regularly and for a decent per-show wage before most agents will take an interest. But even after you are working enough to interest an agent, there are still solid reasons for doing it yourself.

First is the money thing—15 percent is not an insignificant sum. Look at it like this: If your band has any more than five players, then an agent taking a 15 percent cut will make more per gig than any single band member. Don't believe it? Do the math. For grins let's use the example of a six-piece band and a $1,200 gig. First, the agent takes their cut—15 percent of $1,200 is $180. That leaves $1,020 split among six members. Assuming an even split (we'll get into who gets paid what and stuff like "leader pay" in a later chapter), the band cut comes to $170 per person or a bit more than 14 percent of the total. The more players in a band, the bigger the difference between player pay and agent pay.

The second reason for booking yourself is one of control and self-interest. Agents may get you gigs, but they are—like anyone else—usually more interested in their own success than in yours. Booking yourself means never getting talked into a unwanted gig because the agent booked you as part of a package. ("Okay, I'll take Band 'A' for Friday night at full pop, but you gotta get me someone to fill the Tuesday night slot at half the normal rate.") Agents book more than just one band like yours, and the hard truth is that, while all agents have favorites and acts they try to push just because they like them, they get paid regardless of which band they book into a slot. The only way to make sure that someone is giving 100 percent of his or her attention to booking your band is to do it yourself.

Some agents have other self-serving interests. These are the ones who started as successful giggers—booking their own act—and then, after making the right connections and building a clientele over the years, they expanded by starting to book other bands, in addition to their own. As time went on, they continued to book their own act, while passing off secondary gigs to others. Beware of these types of agents who also have their own acts, because you'll never get the first-rate gigs through them. No matter how good you are, even if—*especially* if—you're better than them, they'll always save the best gigs for themselves.

That being said, there are worse things for new bands than to hook up with an established band and take the gigs they can't or won't do.

Yes, it means that they take the "good" gigs and you get the crumbs, but those crumbs can be a valuable source of later gigs. Just keep a couple of things in mind. Don't let the crumbs become your only or even your primary source of work. Doing this puts you in almost an indentured servant role with the established band, and once you're in that role, it's tough to break out of it. Also, have an exit strategy in mind. When the time comes for you to stop taking crumbs because you are getting good gigs on your own, you need to be able to break that tie without alienating your sponsor. Perhaps you'll even be in a position to return the favor by passing a gig or two *their* way.

## What's right with agents

That is not to say that booking yourself is always best. The two biggest problems of the DIY approach are: 1) the time involved; and 2) the simple fact that you *have to* use an agent to get some of the better gigs around, period.

First, the time thing. Keeping a band busy—especially a beginning band—means devoting at least a couple of hours a day to phone calls, research, mailing promo packs, etc. Some giggers are unwilling or unable to make that kind of a time commitment. Bill absolutely hates doing the phone call part of booking, especially cold calls. Plus, he has a day job that takes significantly more than 40 hours a week, and a family and a mortgage. Many weeks, it's hard to even find any time to practice. So an agent is the best route for his band.

And when it comes to good-paying corporate and casual gigs, the vast majority of them are booked by agents. So if you have any desire to do these kind of gigs, you will eventually find yourself working with an agent at least some of the time. Remember our six-piece band example? Well, 14 percent may be less than what the agent is making, but 100 percent of nothing is, well, nothing. Sometimes agents are a necessity. (Side issue: Sometimes the band member who does the booking will take a cut for doing that work. This falls under the whole "leader pay" issue and will be covered at the end of this section.)

The process of booking your own gigs can be broken down into four basic steps: 1) research, 2) canvassing 3) closing the sale 4) follow-up and logistics.

## Research

Do your homework. Check out local clubs, read local arts and entertainment papers, ask questions. Make sure that you are focusing your efforts where they will do some good. Just sending out promo packages blindly, without knowing if your act is appropriate for the venue, is a huge waste of time and money. And it won't make you any friends with bookers. Put yourself in the booker's position for a moment. He or she gets tons of promo kits—anywhere from a dozen to 100 or more per month. Because so many bands *do* mail promo stuff blindly, at least half of what any booker receives is wrong for their venue. The blind mailings just make more work. Worse, they teach the booker that promo kits are a nuisance to be avoided, not a resource that can help their business. Mailing is not the only activity that doesn't work blind. Even when calling a venue, you need to know that you might be right for them before picking up the phone. Calling the booker of the local hip-hop dance club to try to book a gig for your speed metal act will result in little more than getting laughed at.

## Canvassing and closing

When they hear words like "telemarketing" or "cold calling," the first thing most giggers want to do is run away screaming. That's because those words mean you'll be selling something, and most players are trying to avoid that kind of job. That's not surprising; it's a tough gig. There's a lot of pressure, you're dealing with strangers, you don't get paid unless you convince them to work with you. It's almost like trying to make a living as a musician.

Like it or not, getting more paying gigs for a band means learning how to sell. Marina Garcia is a working bass player with a day job selling advertising for a large weekly newspaper. Her sales chops have made her a valuable member of several bands.

■ ■ ■

Playing music is a lot of fun, but it's fun you'll never have outside your garage if you don't treat your band as a business. And selling a band over the phone works the same as selling any kind of product to a potential client. It's a harsh truth, but to a potential client— whether it's an important club owner or someone booking their cousin's wedding—your music is a product. The client's going to buy from another "vendor" unless you can convince them to buy from you.

With that said, the first part of an effective sale will probably be a conversation on the phone. And there are some very definite do's and don'ts when it comes to selling your band on the phone.

Whoever is making the phone calls for your band must keep in mind that the club owner, or the agency contact, doesn't have any other information that tells them who you are and what they can expect from you as a player. They have to make a snap judgment about what kind of person they are dealing with by the sound and tone of your voice. A good phone voice will keep the contact person on the phone longer. Speak smoothly and pleasantly so that the contact person can understand what you're saying. If your drummer is a mumbling, rambling, easily confused stoner who plays the hell out of his kit, let him stick to drumming. This isn't PC, but it's unavoidably true: The person who makes the business calls for your band shouldn't have a heavy accent or speech impediment that makes him hard to understand, and he shouldn't be the guy who gets really nervous when he talks to his mom on the phone.

Also be sure it's someone who can handle rejection. I make 150 to 200 phone calls a day, telling business owners about the newspaper I work for and how they'll benefit from advertising. Out of those 150 to 200 phone calls, I may bring in five new accounts a day. Although I received just five positive responses from all of those phone calls, I know that some the others who didn't respond will keep me in mind. When they hear from me again—and they *will* hear from me again—they will have had a chance to think about my last call, and I'll pick up some clients on the second trip around that said "no" with the first contact.

This is how it'll work for you, too. Don't just give up on those contacts that don't respond to you the first time. Call again in a couple of weeks—politely, professionally. Eventually, many will say, "Send me your demo." If you get bummed out and quit when you hear the first "No," you might as well not bother. Persistence is crucial.

You also need to listen to what the contact person has to say so that you'll know what they need from you. This takes more work than you might think. Before you make your phone calls, plan your conversation. Sit down and think about what you're going to say. Write it down, so you won't blank out if you get nervous. And put yourself in the shoes of the person you're calling: What would you want to know about a band if you were booking them? This will help you prepare for any questions the contact person may have. "Uh, like, I don't know" is not an impressive answer. It's your band—know the answer.

Since persistence is important, you're also going to need to remember whom you've talked to and what they've said. Don't assume you'll remember; a month from now, 10 or 20 or 100 bookers later, you won't.

So write it down. Create a list. Once a week write down 25 agencies or clubs that you think would be interested. Leave a space between each of the names so that you can write down notes about your conversation with the contact person. This will remind you if the person wants a demo sent to them. Or maybe they didn't have time to talk to you at that moment but would like for you to call back at a certain time and day. There will be times when they aren't interested at all, but it's still good to write that down in your notes, because maybe they just weren't interested at that time and may need your style of music later on. This list will save you time and will help you keep track of whom you have called.

Good notes will also help you to develop relationships. Asking for "the guy who does the booking" on your third call to the same club makes you look like you don't know what you're doing.

On your first call, you'll be asking the questions that will start you on your way to a successful business relationship with the club. Find out who books the club, what number he or she can be reached at, and what his or her position is. Are you talking to the owner, or an outside agency? And when can he or she be reached? Getting that contact time is going to save you a lot of hassle and extra calls.

Don't immediately ask if you can play the club. Instead, ask if you can send a press kit. This will set you apart from most of the callers right away—and keep the booker from saying no without knowing anything about your band.

Remember that "we really rock" isn't enough information for the booker to give you a shot. Find out exactly what the club or client needs, and explain how you can meet those needs; this means knowing something about the clubs you call, whenever possible, before you dial the phone.

End with an agreement to send a press kit and the booker's promise that he'll check it out. Many or most press kits go from the mail straight to the round file or end up in a stack that never gets listened to—but you'll be calling back, so don't worry about that.

One week later, call. Never ask "What did you think?" Instead, ask if they got your package. If they don't offer an opinion, ask if they had a chance to check it out and listen to the demo. Never assume. Talk some more about what you can offer. If this is a club gig, do you have a following? How about a mailing list? What can you do to help the club owner make money? If it's a private gig, talk about your experience in this kind of situation. Offer references. The bottom line: Find as many ways as you can to explain what makes you better than the competition.

This is the hardest part of any sales gig. In fact, many large sales organizations have salespeople and closers—the salesperson preps the client, answers questions and, when the time is right, brings in the closer for the kill. You don't have that luxury, so you need to know how to close yourself.

So, you've presented your product, answered the client's questions and, finally, asked for a gig. What's next? There is a saying in the sales field about this crucial moment—"The next one to speak, loses." What that means is that once you have done all of your prep work and asked for the "sale" (in this case the gig), shut the hell up. You won't always get the gig this way, but you stand a better chance.

Selling over the phone isn't easy. But if you have a good phone voice, a strong personality, are not afraid of rejection, and can follow some basic rules, you definitely won't be afraid to pick up that phone. And believe me: As hard as it may be at first, you'll feel pretty good about it when you start landing more paying gigs.

■ ■ ■

## Follow-up and logistics

Once you have "closed the deal" you need to get some basic logistical info on the gig and at least try to get a signed contract. For private party and casual gigs, this should not be a problem, but many club owners balk at putting anything in writing. Keep in mind that their refusal to sign a contract is usually a sign that you're gonna get screwed when it comes time to get paid. (We'll cover contracts in greater depth later in this section.)

The list of questions to ask will vary depending on the circumstances, but here are a few that you will almost always need.

• What time does the band start?
• What time do we end?
• How many sets?
• Do you have a specific time per set in mind or can we determine that ourselves?
• Is there a house PA or should we bring our own?
• If so, is there a soundman?
• Who pays him, the house or the band?
• Where do we load in?
• Is there parking available for the band?
• What time can we begin setting up?
• Are there other bands on the bill? Is there a cover charge?
• How much?
• How many people can we have on our guest list?
• Are there any special requirements we need to know about?

Even after the logistics are handled and the contract signed, at least one follow-up phone call as the gig approaches is a good idea. Just call and say you're looking forward to the gig and just wanted to check and see if anything had come up since your last conversation that you should know about. This will make you look more pro in the eyes of the booker or client and can even derail situations like the dreaded double booking.

When Quint's most recent cover band was just getting their first gigs, they arrived at a restaurant gig excited and ready to play. But another act was already set up—yes, the dreaded double booking. (It happens to everyone sooner or later.) The restaurant manager had screwed up; it was his fault. But rather than making a big deal about it, and getting the booker mad at them, Quint & Company simply turned around and headed home. Frustrated because they were "all dressed up with no place to play," they got a little crazy on the way home. They stopped at another restaurant totally without warning and asked if they could play. Believe it or not, the restaurant manager said yes—and the unplanned stop turned into a regular, paying gig. So don't be afraid to be crazy and spontaneous when trying to land your first gigs.

## The eight types of gigs

While there are many types of musical genres and variations on those genres, there are really only about eight types of gigs that can be further grouped under a couple of general headings. We'll wrap up this chapter by looking at these categories. The point is that hopefully you'll start to get the feeling that there may be many more opportunities for paying gigs in your market than you originally thought.

The two main gig categories are *casuals* and *regular* gigs. Casuals, or *one-offs*, are things like private parties, company functions, and weddings. Some people call them *one-nighters*. Regular or repeating gigs generally mean clubs, bars, restaurants—the kinds of places that feature entertainment regularly and where you can gig more than once. Some gigs that may be seen as one-offs can become regular, if infrequent. For example, Bill plays several festivals and city-sponsored events every year. Though they come around just once every 12 months, they have become regular gigs.

## Clubs versus casuals

Let's get some terms straight before we go any further. We are using West Coast terminology here. Out here club gigs take place in bars or nightclubs, and casuals refer to one-off private functions like weddings, corporate events, and private parties. On the East Coast casuals are often called "club dates," which can get confusing. The main thing to understand is that clubs and casuals might as well be separate planets.

The club booker will usually want to know one thing right away: How many people you can bring in to the club? In times past, bookers knew what kind of acts worked for the audience that frequented their club, and they booked quality acts that fit their parameters. But much has changed in clubland, and these days many club bookers care not a whit about style or even if the band is any good as long as they put butts in seats and beers in hands. On the other hand, casual bookers are not worried about your "draw." They know people will be at the event, so they need a band that fits the vibe, is professional, and knows how to meet the needs of the client. Booking casuals usually means less freedom to do whatever it is that is your "thing." If the mother of the bride wants to hear "Brown-Eyed Girl" for the third time in an hour, you'd better be ready to play it. At a casual gig, the band is usually not the focus of the event and that can mean some major artistic compromises. If that kind of restriction is a problem, stick to clubs. Of course, not being the focus also allows for certain freedoms, so as long as you create the right ambience, you might have a certain latitude in what you play.

Here are the eight basic types of gigs—clubs and casuals—and how to get them.

**Wedding receptions.** These are generally well-paying gigs, although you can't play very loud and you have to have a very conservative and diverse set list. And obviously the competition from DJs is high. Plan on spending some money on nice clothes and regular dry cleaning bills. You'll also have to have some "master of ceremonies" skills leading the first dance, money dances, and other traditions.

Without an agent there are several ways to get these gigs: Put your business cards up at wedding dress shops (or give them to the wedding dress shop owners with the promise of a percentage kickback on referrals). You can do the same with cake/bakery shops and anywhere frequented by people planning to get married. There are also local and regional wedding shows in many cities. Keep an eye out for these events. Attend them; put cards or flyers on cars in the parking lot. You may even find a booking agency with a booth; drop off your promo kit. You should also look in the phone book and contact wedding planners. Give them your promo pack as well and discuss a percentage they can earn for booking you in the weddings they plan. Money talks.

**Bars/clubs.** In many parts of the country this is the bread and butter of the working cover band. If you don't mind the late nights, the smoke, the booze (remember, they aren't drunks, they're "regulars"), then these gigs are for you. In general, the "loudness factor" is not an issue. We can't remember the last time a club owner told us to "turn it down." You should know the prime clubs and bars in your immediate area; use a phone book to locate others in and beyond your region. Weekly arts and entertainment newspapers are another good source for info on clubs that are booking bands.

**Restaurants/coffee houses.** If you're a solo, duo, or trio, then these may be your most viable gigs. In many cities you have hundreds—if not thousands—of possible places to play. The key difference between these gigs and bars/clubs is that generally you're not the main attraction; you are there for background music. So be prepared to play relatively softly and not get much applause. In fact, if you are "too good" you may draw too much attention and too much applause, and this could displease the manager.

There is also a kind of combo class of a bar/club attached to a restaurant, or a restaurant that gets "clubby" after a certain hour. These gigs land between the hard-core boozy atmosphere of most bars and the generally nicer but less fun restaurant gigs. Here, though, as with weddings, you need a greater degree of flexibility, starting with a set or two that lets folks know you are there without scaring off the diners, then gradually ratcheting up the energy as the atmosphere intensifies.

**School/church dances.** These can be good money in certain markets and at certain times of the year (homecoming, prom, etc.). Obviously, people want to dance at these gigs, so your set list should reflect this. Call the main school office number and ask for a contact on the dance or entertainment committee. Generally, there is some type of school committee, composed of students and a faculty advisor, that makes decisions regarding bands and entertainment at these types of functions. Even if you submit a complete promo kit with audio, the committee may want to come visit you at a practice or at another performance. And speaking of schools, you can also contact reunion organizations and committees.

Church dances are tougher. In some parts of the country, bands can stay pretty busy just working church circuits. Bill and Quint both did tons of these gigs in their youth, although the market has gotten tougher and many of these gigs have been taken over by DJs. Be aware that if you take these gigs it will mean watching your volume and checking your lyrics and stage patter for anything that could be deemed inappropriate. But the money can be there. And the gigs generally go from 8 to 11, which can be nice when you are used to 9-1.

**Corporate functions.** Without a booking agent, these are difficult gigs to go after—unless you are well established. When you don't have an agent, these events usually fall into your lap when someone approaches you at another gig: They work for IBM's regional office and think you'd be great for the upcoming Christmas party. This is why you should always be prepared with at least a business card, if not a full media kit. So don't forget "the band briefcase" when you head out to any gig.

These gigs generally pay very well and usually end before midnight, but don't think for a minute that you are the main attraction at a corporate gig. You will have to be extremely flexible in your sets and start and stop times. It is not unusual for a four-hour corporate gig to include two hours or even less of actual playing. On the up side, audiences are generally well behaved (after all, the boss is in the room), you get fed, and like we said before, the pay is good.

**Private parties.** These are good first gigs and can be the source of better paying work than a lot of clubs can offer. Unless you get the gig through a friend or acquaintance, or the client sees you in another venue, well-paying private parties are generally booked by agents. These are gigs where it is important to carry business cards and press kits as they can be the source of future work. (Keep in mind that the card you are handing out may be the agent's. More on this when we talk in depth about agents.) Gigs of this type will almost always require that you carry your own sound system in addition to your personal gear.

**Community events and festivals.** The paying versions of these are tough to break into, but they can be a source of repeat business for many years. The gigs can range from concerts in the park and small community dances to huge street festivals for several thousand people at a time. These are often booked by agents, but sometimes you can get in directly by finding out who in the city government or what local group is putting the event together.

**Niche gigs.** Sometimes gigs can be found—well-paying gigs at that—where you least expect them. For example, we know of a sax player who plays with bunches of jazz and R&B bands but who actually makes a large portion of his income working two-hour daytime shows with a harpist at retirement homes. One of Quint's co-songwriters recently did a gig at a corporate cafeteria. Or how about the guitarist who rocks out on the club scene at night and does children's shows at schools during the day? The key is to keep your eyes and ears and mind open to any and all possibilities.

# AGENTS, BOOKERS, MANAGERS, AND CONTRACTORS

*I have been successfully performing rock and roll more than
30 years. I have had one agent that: 1) didn't lie to me;
2) didn't lie about me; 3) actually worked for me.*

Tom Skidmore

Few subjects will get long-time giggers more animated than the business folks who can literally make or break your efforts to make money making music. Let's start out with some definitions so we have a good understanding of the roles that go along with the names.

**Booker.** Similar to agents, except that the booker is usually an employee (or owner) of the venue or venues he or she books and as such is paid by the venue, not the artist.

**Managers.** Of all of these categories, the role of the manager is the most nebulous. Managers may be many different things to different bands. In some cases they just take care of the business stuff that we all hate. In some instances they may actually book gigs.

**Contractor.** Think of this as the music business version of a construction job, where a contractor hires the workers needed to fulfill the needs of the job. Contractors don't usually work with actual bands, but rather with individual players and singers. Say a client calls, looking for a small jazz combo for a private party. The contractor goes to a list of appropriate players and puts together a group, maybe for just that gig. The contractor may be the leader on the gig as well.

**Agent.** Traditionally, the agent is an independent businessperson who serves as a kind of gatekeeper between musicians and venues, although those lines have blurred a bit in the past decade or so. An agent procures gigs and charges the artist a percentage of the night's pay for his or her services.

## The booker

Now let's get down to reality, starting with the folks you are most likely to run into earliest and most often in your gigging endeavors—the bookers.

Bookers are most often employees of the venues. They may be bartenders who take a real interest in the bands and seem to enjoy dealing with musicians. They could be assistant managers who have been saddled with the job of booking bands on top of their "regular" job and really want nothing to do with you or your band. The booker may even be a local gigger who plays at that venue and books the nights he or she is not playing. Or the situation could be something entirely different.

Sometimes the booker is an independent businessperson who may book bands at a number of different venues. Denise Cogan is a good example. She has taken care of booking music for a variety of clubs in Southern California while also representing a popular regional reggae/soca act called Upstream. Here's what she has to say about bookers:

■ ■ ■

Personally I hate the term "booker." I like "talent buyer" because, after all, we are buying talent for the club. Works three ways. The club pays the booker a flat salary or salary + commission. Or sometimes they pay the booker a commission on what is booked. Bottom line: The booker is just an agent for the venue. You either work from home and go into the venue several times a week, or with the larger venues you go in during the day part-time or certain days of the week to field your calls. Most have set times and days they accept calls.

Why would I book one band over the next? In clubs, generally the owners decide what type of music they want and how much they have for their budget. I like to take chances and give a lot of artists chances as well. But I have to please the club owner, and I am going to follow the rules and the budget so I keep the job. After the artist plays, if the owner does not like them or they do not draw, then generally I am told not to book them again. Not much freedom of choice in these matters for me.

For corporate affairs and private parties, the clients tell me exactly what they want. I pick their brain and find out how much room they have, what style or styles of music they want, how old the crowd is, how many are in the crowd, etc., etc. Then I choose three possible bands for the gig—generally artists I have worked with before, or occasionally a new one. Now my clients will choose one of the packages I mail them. Then I will arrange for them to see the band perform live. If that band is not what they are looking for, then we go back to the drawing board and I submit more promo packs until they find what they need. These gigs pay lots of money, so I don't want to lose these clients. I want them to continue to return to me year after year. I want them to be treated like royalty! So the bands I choose will have to be totally professional, great musicians, and not troublesome at all. Yes, I will have seen the selected band perform more than once, and will know them and trust them with all my heart! They will be on time, they will act professionally, and they will do everything they are supposed to according to the contract I draw up.

My working relationship with the artist is always good because I do not rip artists off. I always make sure they get free parking, food and accommodations, and are treated very well.

Most of my clients come to me by word of mouth and they trust me before even calling me. They also come back year after year for more music. If I send a band out on a private gig and they screw up in the least bit, they will never get another private gig from me again. Sorry, but I cannot take those chances with my business.

■ ■ ■

The biggest difference between gigs from an agent and those procured through a booker is often money. While the agent does not work for and may not even care about your band, he or she does have an incentive to get as much as possible from the promoter or venue as his or her commission is directly based on the amount the band gets paid. The booker, on the other hand, has no such incentive.

Indeed, as an employee of the venue owner or operator, the bookers have every reason to try to get bands to play for as little as possible. Even if the booker is the music-loving/cares-about-the-band type, he or she is generally saddled with a hard budget and has the tough job of getting the best bands possible, provided they will bring people in the door and make the owner money.

## The manager

Next on our list of definitions is the manager. Though this should probably be the last person you deal with, it rarely works out that way. This is because there is almost always someone in the band's general orbit—a friend, a spouse or significant other, a family member, or even a devoted fan—who offers to take over some of the more mundane business duties and soon fancies him- or herself the band's manager. Though it can be tempting to let someone else do some of the grunt work, these situations have been the cause of more than their share of band breakups.

Kenny Kerner is a producer and personal manager who has worked with artists including Gladys Knight and Kiss. Though his advice is tilted toward the needs of original artists, pretty much everything he says here applies to cover bands as well.

■ ■ ■

Most bands, whether they play covers or originals, will have to take care of a certain amount of business in addition to being their charming, creative selves. The first question is, "When do I need some kind of management help?" Here's the answer:

Make a list of all the artistic/creative/band things you need to accomplish—rehearsing, making demos, playing gigs, etc. Call that List A for Artist. Now make a second list with all of the business things you need to take care of—opening a band checking account, booking gigs, interfacing with the industry, etc. Call that List B for Business.

When List B becomes as long as or larger than List A, it's time to at least consider some management help.

Because you are not earning enough to interest a full-time manager or a management company, you might have to enlist the help of a friend or relative. This can be good. Here's a checklist with both the good points and the bad points of this kind of alternative management.

### Good Points
- Having a friend or relative work with you can get work done and free you up to spend more time on your music and your band.
- You save money by being able to pay them lower commissions.
- They are committed to you. They do not manage other bands.
- This makes them feel important so they want to succeed.

### Bad Points
- They have no connections in the industry.
- You are only taking small, baby steps forward.
- Will other band members take your college buddy or uncle seriously?
- They can become mad with power and really believe they are managers.

If you do decide to enlist a relative's services, when you speak with them do not ask them if they will temporarily manage you. Ask if they can *represent* your band for the time being until you become more successful and can attract a real management company. It's okay for Uncle Marvin to be the band rep and to say so in telephone calls. By being honest and above board, you lay the ground rules from the start and there are no surprises and nobody gets hurt. By not using the word "manager" you avoid a problem later.

■ ■ ■

### Contractors

Before we discuss agents, let's look at a person many giggers never deal with, but one you need to know about and understand: the contractor.

A contractor generally works with large venues or businesses that know pretty precisely what they want but don't really care about what act does the entertaining. They don't want to deal with the details. (For example, studio work for movies and TV shows is almost exclusively handled by contractors.) The contractor will generally get a request from a buyer for a specific kind of act, anything from an instrumental surf band to a 17-piece big band to a string quartet to a bluegrass combo. The contractor negotiates all of the details from load-in time to pay rate and then starts looking for musicians to "fill the order."

Sometimes the contractor will deal with a pre-made band, but most often he or she will call individual players until the roster is filled. On many occasions the contractor will also be the leader on the job. "From the musician's point of view, I know of little difference between the function of agents and contractors," says jazz pianist/band leader/contractor/*Jazz Times* columnist Billy Mitchell. "Both provide musicians for specific occasions and needs. The music contractor may deal with more musicians (extras for movies, videos, multiple groups for events, etc.) on a less personal level. The agent may be more aggressive because, while the contractor's profits are usually set by union scales, the agent's profits are determined by what he or she can negotiate. The best way to secure a relationship with either is by demonstrating dependability. You must consistently exemplify preparedness, professionalism, and a positive attitude toward what you do. If a contractor knows that you will: 1) be on time; 2) play the appropriate music; and 3) conduct yourself professionally, then you stand a chance of getting work.

"Just remember that it takes a long time to develop a good reputation … but only a few minutes to blow it," says Mitchell.

## Agents

And finally—agents. They can be your best friend, as in "I have a gig available for the 19th at a private ranch on the beach. It's some kind of convention for single swimsuit models on the make. It's two sets, a full dinner, and the pay is $300 a man. Are you available?" Or they can be your worst enemy, as in "You'll never gig in this town again!" And some agents have the power to actually pull that off.

A couple of other notes about agents: Some states require booking agents to be licensed, regulated, and perhaps even to post some kind of performance bond. Because these requirements can be pretty strict, many biz types who are doing the same thing agents have done for ages will call themselves bookers or even promoters in order to avoid any legal restrictions on their activities and commissions.

Also, while as a working cover band this should not really affect you, you must be aware that the topsy-turvy world created by bands paying to play, playing for free or for "exposure," has resulted in some rather strange arrangements for "agents"—schemes that would have been unthinkable in years past and that skirt at least the intent of both traditional and legal definitions of the word "agent."

About a year ago, Bill was asked to sit on a panel assembled by the San Francisco area branch of the National Academy of Recording Arts and Sciences (the group that does the Grammys) for a Q&A session with local bands. He was more than a bit taken aback when another member of the panel (an "agent" from the Bay Area) explained that because most bands were paid so little for performing their own music, she did not work on a percentage basis, but rather required bands who wanted to work with her to pay a retainer (a set monthly fee) for her services booking gigs that don't pay enough for her to collect a commission.

If anyone offers you this kind of deal, run away just as fast as you can.

## Finding and working with good agents.

Now that we have a handle on who's who and who does what, let's talk about how you find and work with these folks. While—in the interest of brevity and non-convoluted language—we have opted to use the term "agent" throughout this next section, most of the tips and advice apply equally to agents, bookers, and contractors. Keep that in mind as we proceed.

Finding and maintaining a relationship with a good agent is sort of a heaven or hell proposition. If you've got a good agent and your band has a good reputation, then the gigs will flow. But it can and probably will take years to reach that level. So what do you do in the meantime? You try to book yourself as much as possible, but also continue to bang your head against the wall, trying to connect with local agents (and bookers, contractors, etc.) The situation, over a period of time, might go something like this:

As your band starts to try to book itself, it will soon become evident which agents and bookers control which venues and clubs in town. As you try to get through via the phone to club managers, the responses will start to sound the same: "We get all our talent through Bill Nelson," or "All the bands are booked through the Song and Dance Agency." If you're getting a lot of responses like this, don't become totally depressed. We've found in more than a few instances that this is just an easy way for club managers to blow off new bands. It doesn't necessarily mean that all of the talent is booked through a third party—although it could. It's just as likely the manager's way of saying, "I don't have time for any new and unproven talent." So keep the pressure on just a bit before you give in and start approaching the so-called agent (or outside booker).

However, in some cities, a good portion of clubs are truly "locked down" by a single agency (or booker). As mentioned earlier in this chapter, sometimes these bookers also have their own acts, so they obviously keep their own calendar as full as possible. These types have been in the market for years, if not decades, and usually have overblown egos. This is due to the combination of having a successful musical act, as well as controlling the purse strings of many area musicians.

You may be able to work your way into better-paying and more rewarding work, but first you are going to have to eat dirt for a while. This means you'll have to take the lower-paying gigs, the long-distance gigs, the late, late gigs (that end at 2 a.m.), and the last-minute gigs. Remember, this is about dealing with agents' egos. Turn down one gig and you may never hear from them again. It's like they're testing you to see how much you're willing to put up with. Even so, take whatever gigs they offer for the first six months or year. The basic rule is, don't turn anything down, if at all possible. If they're getting good feedback on your performances, it should eventually pay off for you.

Think of it as sort of a pro and minor league baseball leagues situation. The agent is not going to test you directly in the best markets or venues, with his or her most valuable clientele, until you've proven yourself at venues that aren't as important.

A few years ago, Quint was trying to get his new band booked by a relatively controlling agent (who had his own band as well). Quint had made contact, the guy had heard the band's demo, said he liked it, etc. But no gigs were coming. Quint checked in every month or two, until finally the agent called with a St. Patrick's Day gig. There was one catch: He wanted the band to learn a set of Irish songs for the gig. But even with the extra work, the band wasn't going to turn it down. They swallowed their pride and said, "No problem."

(Besides, one of the singers was of Irish descent and already knew some appropriate material.) They learned the songs and prepped for the gig, which was several weeks away.

But the work was far from over. Two days before the gig Quint came down with a severe case of the flu. He was so weak he barely had enough strength to get out of bed. The band considered calling the agent and canceling, but because it was a *first* gig from this agent, they knew that if they cancelled they probably would never hear from him again. They just hoped for the best, that Quint would feel better by the evening of the gig. No such luck. He was still just as sick on gig day. But the band still knew they couldn't cancel out—no matter what. So they gutted it out. Quint dragged himself out of bed, shivering and shaking, and somehow did the gig. The payoff came when eventually more calls came from the agent, including a nice resort town gig.

### Approaching agents

So how do you approach them? Well, it's really no different than using your promo kit and demo CD to approach anyone to book your band. The biggest problem here is that agents really are busy, busy, busy. Plus, as suggested earlier, they sometimes have an ego problem. It's going to take time, professionalism, and patience on your part. For example, you may have to create another demo, especially for agents.

While over-produced, multi-track demos can fool some consumers (brides-to-be, student committees, etc.), they don't fool or impress seasoned bookers and agents; they are more impressed with something raw and real, something that shows how good you really sound live. So create a live demo. You may want to create a video demo as well, if you don't already have one in your promo kit. Agents will rarely come to see you live; when they do show up, you can bet it will be during your worst song or when the crowd is not into it at all. In other words, if they do show up it will be at the *totally* wrong time. So stay in control of the situation by offering to send the agent a live video demo tape of your band.

Here's how a first call to an agent may go down. "Hi, this is Quint Randle, I'm calling from a four-piece band in the area—the Beagles. We've been playing a lot of casual gigs recently. We specialize in classic rock and soft rock. And I'd like to send you out our live demo CD and our promo kit, so you can possibly begin to book us…"

You may get the curt response: "I have nothing available. I have plenty of talent."

The way you'll want to respond to this is: "Great, I can appreciate that. But I'd still like you to hear us for any future consideration."

With that he or she will probably let you send something in. But if they still try to blow you off, just take it in and ask if you can call back in six weeks. (And even if they blow you off again and say you can't call in six weeks, try again in six weeks anyway.)

Now, once they've agreed to have you send them a tape, it's still far from over. The biggest battle is actually getting them to *listen* to your CD and look at your promo material. You will have to keep calling every week or so until they actually listen to your CD and scan your material.

Eventually it will pay off (if they like your sound.) Chances are the way you are going to get your first gig from an agent is by some mistake. Some band is going to call in sick; a client is going to call in with a last-minute gig; the agent is going to get ticked off at one of his or her regular bands—something like that. So just being in a position to get the call (waiting in the wings) is about all you can hope for when you're getting started. But again, with patience and professionalism, eventually you will get your chance.

Now a few items of agent reality. There is an old saying about dogs that even the friendliest canine is only four meals away from being a wolf. It reminds us that, though domesticated now, the dog's nature is that of a predatory carnivore. Same deal with agents. Tom Skidmore, the band leader who started this chapter continues:

■ ■ ■

The first thing a band needs to learn is that the typical agent/booker/contractor doesn't care about you. At all. I know he told you he loves you and was a musician himself and would never treat you the way other agents treated him. He's lying. You are a product. There is a never-ending supply of product. There is a finite supply of buyers. He's concerned about:
1) his money;
2) his money;
3) what the buyer wants;
4) his money...
10,036) you and your band.

Do not believe anything he says completely. At a minimum he's putting a spin on it. At worst it's a complete lie. Now, he comes by it honestly. How many times have you lied to the agent? Is the band really able to pull off its song list? Do you sound like your demo? Are the people in your promo pic the same people as the ones onstage now? Can you really cut that tux job at the country club as well as that rowdy club job?"

■ ■ ■

Tom's comments may seem harsh, but he is pretty much on target. It's not that agents are evil; it's just that their interests and yours only line up occasionally, and you need to understand that in order to not get the short end of the relationship.

Here is a hint to get on the good side of an agent forever just by doing what you should do in the first place. When you first book a gig with an agent, make sure to ask him or her for a supply of agency business cards. This is so you can hand out the agent's card to anyone who approaches you at the gig who is interested in booking the band. Show allegiance to your agent and he or she will ... well, may ... return the favor. Even if you book yourself most of the time and only occasionally work with agents, the proper "gigging etiquette" is that if someone approaches you about another gig while you are playing an agent-booked gig, that potential client should be referred to the agent. But because almost no one actually follows this rule, letting the agent know you plan to do so is a sure-fire way to help cement the relationship.

That being said, this kind of referral to the agent is a professional courtesy, and you do it only for gigs that were booked by that agent. Which brings us to perhaps the most important rule when dealing with agents: Never under any circumstances sign an "exclusive" contract with an agent. Sure, being able to say you are under contract with an agent may seem cool or make you feel like a real music biz type, but this kind of contract *will* hurt you. An exclusive agreement with an agent means the agent has little incentive to hustle gigs for you; after all, you have no where else to go. Exclusive agreements also can—and have—been used as a way to quash competition.

It works like this: Say you have started an up-and-coming dance band and are starting to book some gigs that might ordinarily go to another band that has been around longer and that you are in direct competition with. That band's agent approaches you and says he can get you more and better gigs but he only works with bands on an exclusive arrangement. Flattered and sure you'll be this agent's No. 1 band, you sign. You get a few gigs from this agent, but the bigger and better gigs are still going to that other band. That's because the agent never *intended* to get you better gigs; he just wanted you out of the way so he could protect that other band. (Oh, you didn't know he was married to the keyboard player? Guess you should have done some more homework.) Because you signed an exclusive booking agreement, you can't take gigs from other agents even if they are offered and, depending on the contract language, you may not even be able to book yourself.

There may be times when you have to sign an agreement giving an agent the exclusive right to book you at certain gigs or certain venues. This is pretty much unavoidable, so just be very careful that the language of the contract is very specific and very limited; if you have any doubts at all, have it read by a lawyer. For example, there may be a chain of restaurants in your area, all represented by a single agent. In order to get into these venues you may have to agree not to approach any of the other restaurants in this chain on your own.

Another example: Back when they were starting out, both Bill and Quint played in different bands for an agent who booked a circuit of well-paying church dance gigs in the Southern California area. Once a year this agent would hold an all-day showcase for his bands. He would invite the folks responsible for booking bands at the various dances to his studio, where each band would do a five-to-seven-minute set (usually a medley of four or five tunes) and the dance reps would see 15-20 bands in the space of a few hours. As many as 100 gigs would be booked that afternoon, with contracts signed and deposits paid to the agent. In order to be a part of the showcase, all the bands had to agree that anyone who saw them at the showcase and wanted to book them would be referred to the agent.

To wrap up this chapter we want to share one other thought with you: Agents are human beings. In many instances they are just putting on a front, sort of like the wizard in *The Wizard of Oz*. They make all kinds of noise, but in the end they are frail creative types just like the rest of us. Remember Quint's story earlier in this chapter, the one about the agent the band was so worried about that they did the gig even when Quint should have been home in bed? Well, months later, the band had started hosting an open mic night at a local restaurant. And who do you think showed up a few times to play there? The agent! The curtains had fallen, and the wizard was gone. He was just as vulnerable as many of the other musicians in town, just as willing to share his original songs with the local community. The agent had gone from being a curt, gruff voice on the phone, blowing off a new local band, to a fellow songwriter.

Now that you have met and know the enemy—sorry, bad joke— it's time to explore the world of weapons. In this case, that means contracts.

For some links to booking agency sites, go to www.covergigs.com.

**BIZ 4**

# CONTRACTS AND THE DOTTED LINE

*A contract is not only a way of legally protecting yourself, it is also a show of good faith on both the band's and club's part that they are willing to work hard for each other, and that a relationship is being built on trust. We don't always get what we're worth, but a good way to help make sure you get something for all your hard work and sacrifice is to get signed contracts.*

Marc T. Van Patten

The whole premise underlying this chapter is, "It's great to get the gig—but do you really have one? And will you really get paid, or paid what you think you're going to get?" While these apply to *you* trying to get the person hiring your band to sign a contract, it may be the other way around: You must know enough to sign (or not sign) a contract that is being offered to you. Contracts are there to protect you, but they are also designed to protect the contractor (the person paying the bill.) And obviously, the contract will tend to favor whoever created it.

If you present a 15-page contract to the local bar manager in Smithsville, he or she is going to balk. But if you can't get him or her to sign a one-page letter of agreement stating in a few lines when you will play and what you will be paid, then you should probably be the one doing the balking.

We're not attorneys; far from it. Because of that, you will find in this chapter, more than in any other place in this book, input from experts. But this discussion of contracts is not intended to substitute for the advice of a good attorney. For anything beyond a page or so, or anything that involves a significant amount of money or time, you will definitely want to consult an attorney. What we're trying to do with this chapter is educate you so you'll be able to:

1) Create and present a *basic* gig contract or cover letter;
2) Sign a *basic* contract that has being offered by someone else;
3) Know when it's time to consult an attorney;
4) Know some simple questions to ask as well.

In many instances it's simply a matter of creating a simple letter of understanding, an understanding of services offered for a specific payment. It's just a matter of "getting something in writing." In other instances you will be modifying a more complicated document—an American Federation of Musicians (AFM) contract, for example. Again, in more serious situations you'll want to consult an attorney. So let's start with the basics.

### What they are and what they are for

A contract is nothing more than an agreement between two or more parties—in this case your band and whoever is hiring you—that lays out the work to be done, the compensation and manner of payment, and any details specific to that gig. The contract can be as simple as a letter of agreement that lays out the name of the venue and band, date and time of the performance, and agreed-upon payment amount and method. Or it can get more complex and include things like the type of music to be played, volume restrictions, and gear and technical requirements.

A written contract should follow some kind of accepted template. Several years ago, Stephan Eason wrote about what a basic contract should include. His advice still holds up.

■ ■ ■

It's 1:44 a.m., and you're finishing up your last set at the Cheap But Sleazy Lounge. It hasn't been the best of nights, but the worst is yet to come. You play your last song, and turn to put your guitar down. Out of the corner of your eye, you see Rip (the owner of this fine establishment) counting up the door receipts. You wait until he's finished, then stroll nonchalantly over to collect your pay. To your utter amazement and horror, Rip informs you that "certain deductions" are to be made from your fee. Low patronage. Drinks for the band. Too long a break between songs. Didn't play the right kind of music. And so on.

Being the diplomatic type that most musicians are, you politely inform Mr. Rip that you are not to blame for any of these problems, and most important of all, you had an agreement. After a short but heated discussion, you walk back to the band with the bad news that not only is nobody getting paid tonight, but also everyone has to pitch in for gas to make it home. Congratulations. You have just encountered the worst night of your life. The sad fact is, this scenario could probably have been avoided if you had used a contract.

**Sign here**

*Contract.* The word conjures up all kinds of reactions, from "We can't afford to have one made" to "How do you get one?" If you're in the business to make money, or at least to not lose money, you can't afford not to have a contract. There's nothing magical or mystical about one, and it can be as simple or as complex as you want it to be. However, certain things need to be in every working musician's contract.

First, the contract should have some means of identifying you (*i.e.*, the Artist) and the person or party paying for your services (*i.e.*, the Purchaser), along with the date that the contract is made. This is in addition to the date the contract is for. Immediately following, a clause should be inserted that says whatever musicians are to be used—whether they have been chosen or not—are to be bound by the contract, and that they agree to render services under the person representing the band that signs the contract. Some groups use different musicians for different jobs, so if a person is hired for a specific job, he or she is bound by this clause to uphold the contract. Believe me, it's not as bad as it sounds.

Next, you need to insert some blanks that will be filled out, such as the address, date(s), and time(s) of the engagement, along with a "special conditions/instructions" clause. This enables you or the purchaser to list various needs, such as "the band shall be set up by 6:00 p.m." Again, just leave a few lines of blanks to fill in as needed.

A space for "full wage agreed upon" should come next, followed by spaces for "deposit" and "balance of $_____ to be paid at end of engagement." This way, should the purchaser make a deposit (which is advised, when possible) toward the amount agreed upon, it can be listed, along with the balance to be paid. (Note: When using booking agencies, you use their contract, which usually asks for a fairly large deposit. This covers the majority, if not all, of their commission. In cases where the deposit exceeds the commission due an agent, that exceeding portion is given to the band after the engagement.)

### The good stuff

Now comes the fun part. Various clauses can be inserted here; *i.e.,* "A bowl of M&Ms with the brown ones removed will be placed in the band's dressing room." (Don't laugh, it's been done.) However, a more down-to-earth approach is recommended. Again, certain things need to be included, such as:

*1. The Leader shall, as agent of the Employer, carry out instructions as to selection and manner of performance.*

*2. The Leader shall at all times have supervision, direction, and control over the services he is rendering, and he expressly reserves the right to control the manner, means, and details of the performance of services to fulfill the entertainment requirements.*

Let's take a look at these two clauses. The first says that the artist signing the contract will act as liaison between the purchaser and the band. If the purchaser wants something, he will tell the bandleader, who in turn will carry it out. The second clause says that the bandleader shall have control at all times of what the band is doing, and how they are doing it. This is a big responsibility, not to be taken lightly. Even though this clause gives the band control, it doesn't give the group the right to disregard everyone else's wishes. If the people who hired you want something, do your best to give it to them. Remember, if they like you, chances are good they'll have you back.

*3. Artist's obligations are subject to detention or prevention by sickness, death, accident, strikes, labor difficulties, riots, civil tumult, natural disasters, means of transportation, acts of God, or other conditions beyond the control of Artist.*

Whew! This clause covers you in case somebody in the band gets sick, or the equipment truck breaks down. In other words, if something happens outside of your control that either causes you to be late to a job or to have to cancel, then you will not be held liable. However, remember two things: 1) You don't play, you don't get paid; 2) This clause doesn't give you the right to be slack and skip out on a job because your lead vocalist just had a fight with his wife. Even if you're only going to be five minutes late, contact the purchaser if at all possible. If they're left to guess, they'll probably assume the worst.

*4. Employer shall be liable for any and all damages to the Artist's instruments or equipment caused by Employer, business invitees, employees, or by the negligence thereof.*

This clause puts all the liability on the part of the purchaser if someone at the job (other than the band) damages any of the band's equipment. If you break your keyboard stand while tearing up a solo, it's your problem. However, if Patty Partygirl pours beer into a monitor while trying to request a song, the purchaser pays. A good rule of thumb to follow here is this: When something happens, stop right there (if possible) and tell the purchaser. You may be able to continue, but disagreements concerning problems may arise later if they aren't at least noted as soon as possible.

*5. If this contract is canceled by Employer without written consent of Artist prior to scheduled engagement, then any deposit made shall be forfeited, and full wage shall be due immediately.*
Self-explanatory.

*6. Employer, in signing this contract himself, or in causing the same to be signed by a representative, acknowledges his authority to do so, warrants that he is of legal majority, and hereby assumes full responsibility and liability for the amount (full wage agreed upon) stated herein, plus any fees and costs (including Attorney's fees in the maximum amount authorized by law) incurred in collecting the full wage agreed upon.*

This not-so-simply states that whoever signs the contract on the part of the employer is legally able to do so, and makes himself liable for the band's fee. In the event that the Artist has to go through legal channels to collect, the Employer will be liable for all legal fees and court costs.

*7. Employer must sign and return all copies of this contract, along with the deposit, for Artist to guarantee appearance.*

*8. Both parties agree that this contract is made and subject to the State of (your state here), and may be enforced in an appropriate court of law.*
Again, it means just what it says.

Finally, put blanks at the bottom where both you and the purchaser can sign, and be sure to include addresses and phone numbers for each. Put it all together, and you've got a contract! A word of advice: Check with your local booking agency, musician's union, music stores, and other bands before jumping into a contract. Laws vary from state to state, so talking with a lawyer or someone at a legal clinic can help. A wise songwriter once said, "Lessons learned are like bridges burned, you only need to cross them but once." Don't get burned.

As if you want even more on "getting it in writing," here are some more tips from another person who knows. Ken Biedzynski is an entertainment lawyer based in New Jersey (he also plays drums in a local cover band). A couple of years ago he answered a letter from a reader about cover band contracts:

*Question: I play in a pretty successful cover band. For now, we really don't have any big aspirations to record or write original music. However, we are starting to play better gigs for larger venues and crowds. Although we never used to ask for or sign performance contracts, that's now changing because of the quality of our gigs as well as the money we are starting to get. What should we be watching out for?*
Jan Mitchell
Via email

Answer: This is an excellent question because all too often everyone overlooks the performance, or "engagement," contract. Although I understand that musicians want to play, if you are not getting paid because you don't have a contract (or you have a lousy one), I don't think your enthusiasm will last too long. And because some people don't pay close attention to these contracts, they all too often wind up in court because they are lacking critical terms or they are drafted poorly. In the end, the expense to litigate is always greater than that of putting together a well-drafted contract.

Here are some thoughts on performance or engagement contracts. First, it is critical that you have a lawyer draft or review your contract. (I strongly discourage oral contracts). Whether you're a band or venue, this usually isn't too expensive, and for the most part it may be a one-time expense because in situations like yours you can probably continue to use the same format over and over again, with some modifications. Another reason to consult an attorney is so that you understand your rights and, particularly, what laws apply. For example, if you agree to go play in another state, you want to make sure that the law of your state applies, not that of the other state. If you overlook this point you may have to go litigate your matter in another state (or worse, defend a lawsuit there).

Now, getting to the contract itself, let me give you some basic tips. First, make sure you actually get the contract signed! Do you know how many times people come into my office and tell me they want to sue someone over an engagement contract, and then when I ask to see the contract I notice that it is not signed by all parties to it? Too many times.

Another tip. Make sure you type into the agreement the person's name who is signing the contract. Do you know how many times I have handed to me a signed contract (when that happens!) but no one can tell me who signed it on behalf of the other party? Too many times.

I understand that some people do not like contracts, and deals can suddenly change when they are reduced to writing. Even so, don't back down. Make sure the contract is signed before you play, and type the person's name into the contract so there is no dispute who signed it. Of course, also make sure the terms are good for you.

As to the essential terms, I start with the obvious. First would be the name of the band and the venue. Be careful about listing specific members only because I sometimes run into the situation where a party will bargain for a certain performer, and when that person doesn't perform there is a problem because the purchaser claims that he specifically bargained for a certain performer.

Next, make sure to state how long you are required to perform (*i.e.*, sets and times) and how you are to get paid. Also, remove subjective language in which the venue reserves the right to act on its "opinion" or "discretion" related to your performance.

List specifics about load-in times and sound and lights, depending on what the venue offers and, more importantly, what you need. A sound check is not the time to sort out disputes about equipment. There are other "frills" provisions you should also consider. For example, do you want a certain number of complimentary tickets or a guest list, security, or amenities? If so, put that into the contract. These items typically belong in a rider as they are very specific to the venue.

Finally, one of the more important concerns is the default provision. A "default" is when one of the parties to a contract fails to perform. For example, the venue or the band cancels at the last minute. Now what? The contract should provide for a remedy in the event of a last-minute cancellation. In most states this provision is called a "stipulated damages" clause.

A good contract not only protects your rights as a performer, but it also should clearly spell out your rights to help either avoid litigation or make it as smooth as possible if it occurs.

■ ■ ■

## How to get a club owner to use one

All that theory sounds great, but how do you get a club owner to sign one? Tom Skidmore, a *Gig* reader from Jacksonville, Florida, offers this advice: "Don't make a big deal about it or act apologetic about presenting a contract to the buyer. It's a fact of the business and he expects it. If he's screwing you around about it, it's just a power trip."

People who book you for private gigs will almost always expect a contract, but clubs can be more problematic. Tom has hit on the most basic approach to getting a venue owner to use a contract: Just act as if you assume he will. At the end of your conversation that ends in a booking, say "I'll put a contract in the mail. Should I just send that to the club?"

At this point one of two things will happen: The booker will tell you to send the contract or he or she will say something like "we don't use contracts." In the latter case, your reply should be something like, "We have a very simple contract that we always use. It just lays out the date and time of the gig and the payment amount that we have agreed on. Why don't I just send it out? You can take a look at it and let me know if you have any problems with anything there."

If at this point the booker still insists that he or she never signs contracts then you should seriously consider turning down the gig. As Marc T. Van Patten reminds us, "Some club owners downright loathe the idea of a band being able to legally recoup losses incurred by shady deals or penny-pinching managers. If they won't sign, chances are they know they have done some dishonest dealing in the past and are afraid to enter into a legal arrangement." It may seem harsh, but the club booker or agent who will not sign a contract is someone with whom you really don't want to do business. It's that simple.

**BIZ 5**

# MONEY AND OTHER FUN STUFF

*If your music involves any commercial activity (i.e., CDs, tickets, merchandise, etc.), lose all anti-business attitudes in order to observe and incorporate any sound and honest business practices that fit your situation in order to maximize your sales in any of these areas.*

Malcolm Hunter

Outside of the great artistic and business training they provide, the main reason we decided to focus on cover bands with this book is that we wanted to show beginning giggers that it really is possible to make money making music. Your friends who insist on playing only *their* music are unlikely to attain the stardom that they seek. It's like the guy who plays roulette—the game in the casino with the worst odds to begin with—and insists on playing all of his chips on a single number. Reaching that pinnacle of superstardom is like that except that the odds are not just 32-1 but more like $32^{10}$-1. Going the cover band route does not ensure success, but it does, at least, make it a bit more likely.

In this chapter we will examine some of the issues that actually making money will raise, including setting prices, opening a band checking account, paying taxes, and the dreaded pay-to-play scam.

### How much to charge

So you're ready to land a paying gig, but how much should you charge? Well, be realistic, but don't undersell yourself. Talk to other working musicians. What does the club you are trying to get into usually pay? What is the going rate for weddings in your area? Research what the market will bear. For example, if you want to find out how much wedding reception gigs are paying in your area, have a friend call a few bands or agents. Have them pretend they are a potential client trying to get an idea of a budget for an upcoming event.

Setting prices is a great example of the fine art of negotiation—a subject about which hundreds if not thousands of books have been written and one that we can't cover in any real depth here. But here are a few tips:

*Get an idea of the budget* before offering a price. If you have done enough homework, you may have this info long before it is time to discuss price. If not, try this: If the client asks "How much do you charge?" answer with "It depends on the type of gig, the location, and some other things. What's your budget?"

No matter what you are charging, *sound like you are giving the client a screaming deal.* If the budget is $800, start out by saying you usually charge $1,200 for this kind of gig but may be able to take less for this particular gig.

If the client is cagey about his or her budget, then *start high.* You can always come down in price, but it is near impossible to go up.

*Don't be afraid to ask for too much*—especially for private and corporate functions.

*Don't take cheap gigs forever.* It's one thing to go low in the beginning, but remember this truth: You will never be a $1,500 band if you keep on taking $300 gigs to keep your chops up.

### Taking it to the bank

While many bandleaders pay all expenses—including gig pay—from their own personal checking account, there are some good reasons to consider opening an account in the name of the band.

First, when you are handed a check for a gig at 3 a.m., and the person who signs the check left hours earlier, and the check is made out to the name of the band instead of an actual person, you won't have to worry about how you are going to cash it.

Next, having a band account just makes you more "real" in the eyes of business people you will work with and even other band members because along with the band checking account comes other logical stuff, like tracking your income and expenses in a computer program such as Quicken. All this makes it easier to tally income and expenses at tax time.

Finally, there are some purely logistical reasons to avoid running band stuff through your own account—like the first time a check for a gig bounces (and it *will* happen eventually), and you have to worry about your rent check clearing as a result. Opening a band checking account will probably require you to file some type of DBA (doing business as) license, so contact your local government. Your bank or savings and loan will be able to point you in the right direction as well.

### There's one for you, 19 for me

If you are making money—any money—playing music, then you will have to pay taxes on it. We strongly recommend that you have a qualified tax person prepare your returns. There are just too many potential pitfalls, challenges, and outright disasters waiting for you if you try to do it yourself and find that you have crossed over that fine legal line.

The biggest thing to remember when it comes to taxes is that you must keep good, organized records of income and expenses. Here is some general tax wisdom, courtesy of *Gig* contributor Chris Bray:

■ ■ ■

Taxes can be a real a headache. But faced head-on, tax time can be dealt with pretty quickly.

If you pay the people in your band, the threat of headaches goes double for you: You owe them an accounting of the money they've earned throughout the year. You also owe the Internal Revenue Service—and the state tax agency in the state where you played the gigs and made the money—the same information. This will make you wonder if this "taking responsibility" thing is really all that great an idea, but never mind. Somebody has to be the grownup; it might as well be you. Just think how proud your folks will be.

The bottom line is actually pretty simple. If you've paid band members as independent contractors—and most of you will have, but more about that later—then you owe them all a form called a

*1099-misc.* (The "misc." stands for miscellaneous; the abbreviation makes this a particular type of 1099 form.) But you don't have to worry about it if the player in question made less than $600 from you all year long. If they did top the $600 figure, get that form to them.

There's a deadline, too. Players should usually get 1099 forms no later than January 31.

There's also an important second part: You need to provide copies of the 1099 to both the IRS and the appropriate state tax agency. If you earned all your gigging money in Iowa, for example, the state of Iowa gets a copy of the 1099—even if you all live in Nebraska. If a player made more than $600 in several states, then several states will be getting 1099 forms—you have to pay taxes to a state if you make money inside its borders. (If this applies to you, you should be talking to a good tax accountant; tax liabilities across several state lines cry out for someone who really knows what he's doing.) The deadline for getting the 1099 to the tax agencies is usually February 28.

There can be serious consequences if you ignore your responsibility to provide 1099s. If you don't send 1099 forms to the players who earned money gigging with you, and send them in time to meet the deadline, you can face a $50 federal fine for each player—and state fines that depend on which state you're talking about. Fines for missing or ignoring deadlines for getting copies of the forms to the IRS or state agencies vary greatly, depending on how badly you miss the deadline.

If you've been paying your band members as employees—and very, very few of you will have been doing that—then you owe each of them a W-2 form, and you owe the IRS and the appropriate state tax agency copies. The deadlines are the same as for 1099 forms: February 1 for players, February 28 for the tax agencies. The fines are the same, too, so be careful.

Don Roberts, the IRS spokesman who provided us with most of this information, took care to point out that some much more serious fines await a responsible band leader who makes all the deadlines but gets a more important question wrong. The real issue, Roberts says, is, "Were they independent contractors, or were they employees?"

An *independent contractor* is someone you pay without withholding taxes or paying the several different obligations that fall to employers—an extra share of Social Security tax, for example. An employee costs you more money, since you pay extra taxes based on the amount of money the employee earns; you also take money out of his or her pay throughout the year to send to the state and federal tax agencies.

And you can't just decide to treat a player as an independent contractor because it's easier for you; there are some very specific conditions that have to be met to make a player an indie.

The IRS judges whether a taxpayer is an independent contractor or an employee using a sort of matrix, with several factors that overlap and interplay. You can find this pattern of rules in the agency's Publication 15-A, also known as the *Employer's Supplemental Tax Guide*.

Among the factors are:
- "Whether the business has a right to direct and control how the worker does the task for which the worker is hired."
- "The extent to which the worker has un-reimbursed business expenses."
- "The extent to which the worker makes services available to the relevant market."
- "The permanency of the relationship."
- "Written contracts describing the relationship the parties intended to create."
- "How the business pays the worker."

We'll say this again: If you have any doubts about this stuff, you should be working closely with a tax professional to keep yourself out of hot water. There are also several other ways to get more information. The IRS tax assistance hotline is a toll-free number, 800-829-1040. (Be prepared to spend some time on hold.) The IRS also has a Web site, at www.irs.ustreas.gov/, with all kinds of information. The catch is that there's so much information it becomes kind of not so fun to find exactly what you need, but still it's worth spending the time.

Many of the most important IRS publications—but not all of them—are directly available on the agency's Web site, in the html format; go to www.irs.ustreas.gov/prod/forms_pubs/pubs/index.htm to browse through the list.

Finally, you'll need copies of the 1099 and W-2 forms themselves, in triplicate so you can send copies to everyone who should get them. These are easily available at any office supply store. A 24-pack of 1099 forms, for example, was selling for $4.49 when we stopped in to an office supply store in Los Angeles recently.

And that's it. Now there's nothing left to do but the work.

One of the main reasons to make sure you file those 1099 forms is that the amount you pay out to other band members gets deducted from the amount you owe taxes on. If you try to be the cool guy and don't 1099 your band mates, you will be on the hook for the tax on the entire amount that the band earned. This is a bad thing.

Lots of other expenses are deductible too, like mileage to and from gigs, gear, stage clothes, and guitar strings—but remember a few things: 1) if you have more deductions than you have income, you raise a nasty red flag with the IRS and may get audited; 2) you must keep good records with receipts for all expenses in case of an audit; and 3) get yourself a good tax person. How many times have we said that now? Is it starting to sink in?

## Pay-to-play

Finally, we come to a practice that has sprung up in many clubs — *pay-to-play*. Being in a working cover band, you should not have to deal with it much, as it applies mostly to wannabe rock stars desperate to get on a stage. But you need to know about it in case the ugly and insidious practice should ever rear its head, and also because the practice has seriously depressed the pay scale for live music in many parts of the country. You need to know the enemy in order to defeat it. Here is something Bill wrote on the subject for *Bass Player* magazine.

Would you work a day job where you had to pay the owner for the privilege of working, and then hope enough people came into the business on that day so you could get paid? Unfortunately, loads of otherwise smart musicians do just that every day. It's called pay-to-play, and it is one of the notoriously scummy music business' scummiest practices.

There are several pay-to-play scams and formats going, but the most common is probably the "ticket pre-sell." It works like this: Club owner or booker gives a band a date and the pitch begins. "We expect our bands to bring in at least 100 people for a Tuesday night show. Tickets cost ten bucks each, but we sell them to you for just five. You sell the tickets for $10 and you make $500."

This may sound reasonable to someone outside the business, but we all know that bands—especially new, original bands—are more likely to have monkeys fly out of their butts than to get 100 people to pay ten bucks each to see them in a club in a questionable area of town on a Tuesday night. The end result is that the band sells maybe 25 tickets at five bucks each and gives the rest away, leaving them $375 in the hole.

If you are getting onstage and playing music in front of people, you are all but certainly—protestations of purely artistic intent notwithstanding—looking to get paid. In a situation like this, not only are you not putting any money in your pocket, you are actually finishing the gig more impoverished than when you began. That sucks but it goes way deeper.

In L.A., where I live and the city where pay-to-play is probably the most common (although rumor has it that the practice actually started in San Francisco comedy clubs), pay-to-play has all but killed the chance to play music in a club and actually get paid. Even the local joints where a cover band could get a weekend gig for decent bread have gone the three-bands-on-a-bill-and-none-of-'em-get-paid route. A few club owners have figured out that while this system might mean no risk for them, it is failing to develop much in the way of repeat and regular business. These clubs have gone back to actually paying bands, but the pay scale has been so depressed by pay-to-play that the guarantee for a four-hour gig is no better in the year 2002 than it was in 1980.

The worst part is that it almost never works. (I want to say never, but there is the off chance that it has worked for someone, some-where, sometime.) I know a lot of bands, a lot of great bands. I know bands that have been signed to major labels. I know bands that have gotten signed and actually sold records and made money. Not one of them got there by playing pay-to-play showcases because the owner swore that label A&R types frequent the club. Not a sin-gle one. Anyone who tells you that paying to play on their stage will further your career is lying to you.

**What can you do about it?**

The first thing you can do is refuse to participate. The most important thing you can do is to expand your thinking. No one says you have to play at any specific club. There are always other places to play.

Although I really hate to see musicians play for free, it is better than paying to play. Try not to do it, though, because it hurts all musicians. When you play for nothing, it drags down the pay scale for everyone. Also, playing for the door, while far from an ideal situation, is better than playing for free or paying to play. Here are some ideas for avoiding both.

**1. Take cover gigs.** Playing covers and throwing in the occasional original tune is a tried and true method for getting your music to potential fans.

**2. Look for alternative venues.** Clubs are not the only game in town. Lots of cities sponsor concerts in the park during summer months. Lots of high schools and colleges will bring bands in to play lunchtime shows. I used to play a regular gig at a swap meet. The pay was decent and audiences were more than willing to hear the occasional original. My *Gig* magazine contributors—all working players—did everything from cruise ships to retail grand openings.

**3. Grow your own.** If you must go out of pocket for a gig, get several bands together, rent a warehouse, and have a party/concert. You may still lose money, but you won't be enriching a slime-bucket club owner in the process.

Finally, keep in mind that there are a lot of folks in the biz who will say you have to do pay-to-play gigs. They'll tell you it is how business is done and that it's just part of paying your dues. They're wrong. Pay-to-play is a sucker's game. Just say "No way, dude."

■ ■ ■

Money, while it can cause headaches, is not the only potential pitfall for you to avoid. Let's move on and take a look at some important intra-band issues.

## BIZ 6

# INTRA-BAND ISSUES

*As the name of my band, Nailing Gell-O, testifies, keeping personnel in a band together and happy for the long haul is like "nailing Jell-O to the wall" ... in other words, very difficult.*

Dave Robinson

Throughout the chapters in the Biz section of this book, we've been primarily concerned with marketing and business issues *outside* the band. However, in this chapter we'll look at some of the business-oriented issues you will probably be confronting *within* the band on a regular basis. These range from deciding if and when to pay yourself more as a band leader/manager to making decisions without making enemies to firing a band member—and much more. While some of these issues may seem a bit picky when you are first starting a band, several years later they can mushroom into major crises. You lose enough sleep with those late-night gigs; you don't need to lose any more on account of personnel problems.

### Follow the leader

Have you heard this joke: "Mommy, I want to be a musician when I grow up!"

"Now dear, you can't have it both ways."

"Bandleaders tend to be the Designated Grownup," says Kevin Johnsrude of the Nettles. "Your bandleader will be the bossiest band member who books all your gigs, writes your set lists, collects the money after the gig, and always has spare batteries for the guitarist's stomp boxes. Be nice to this person or you will soon find out how much work it is to keep a band together and gigging. If it's going to be a democratic band, then everyone has to pull their weight or the slackers will find themselves gig-less. Responsibility is power."

It has been said that a band is a lot like a marriage and, just as money issues are often at the root of failed marriages, disagreements about money have split up bunches of bands. On the surface, it appears simple: The gig pays $500 and there are five people in the band, so everyone gets $100. If all of the non-musical duties of running a band are being evenly split among the membership, then it can be that simple. But if there is someone in the band who provides a rehearsal space, owns and maintains the PA, and books the gigs, is it fair for that person to get paid the same as someone who shows up for gigs and rehearsals but does nothing else?

Full-time musicians who are members of the Union are used to differing pay scales, as for most gigs the set amount for a bandleader is 50 percent higher than any other individual musician. But, especially in the apparently more egalitarian rock world, some of us have yet to embrace the fact that he who does more work should get more pay.

For example, up until a few years ago, even as a longtime band bandleader, Bill always split gig money evenly despite the fact that the description above fits him pretty well. Finally, after a string of low-paying gigs, he decided to take $5 off the top of everyone's cut to cover the cost of booking—phone calls, mailing, etc. He was genuinely shocked when two members of the band had fits over the arrangement.

That was the point when he stopped dividing gig money evenly and started taking leader pay. Note that in the real world leader pay can also be less than what others in the band make. As leader, Bill often takes a smaller cut than anyone else if he books a gig that doesn't pay as well as it could. In fact, in many bands there are two, three, or four different levels of pay, depending on the contribution of each member. One L.A. jazz venue we know of has separate scales for the leader, the singer, and the "side" players. There are plenty of pro bands out there in which a small "core group" makes most of the money while other players are paid smaller salaries.

But this can cut both ways. For example, as a Union member Bill tries to pay other Union members in his band no less than minimum scale regardless of what the job pays. This can sometimes mean that the rest of the band makes a little less, and that Bill make less still. On the other hand, on well-paying gigs, he pays everyone a decent amount and takes that 50 percent leader bonus for himself. It balances out those times when he takes less and helps cover some of his costs as the band leader. The sticking point here is often explaining differing pay scales to other band members. How do you avoid this turning into a kind of confrontation? By avoiding the problem altogether. In other words, if you are the leader, never talk about how much the gig pays total. Talk about what it pays per player.

The bottom line is that unless it's a totally democratic band, with everyone sharing equally in business and marketing responsibilities, it's no one's business how much money anyone else makes. Think about "straight" businesses. When you report for work, does the owner or manager introduce you to everyone else by telling you how much each gets paid? And didn't we already tell you that running a band is the same as running a business? Get the connection?

### The PA problem

Every working band has to have at least one PA system. While you may start out by renting in the early stages of band development, at some point a system (or parts of a system) will have to be purchased. But who should buy it? After all, there are players who seem to think that they don't have a responsibility to help buy the PA system because they don't sing.

Here are three approaches to PA ownership that can help avoid problems in the future when someone leaves the band—for whatever reason:

**1. Everyone buys pieces.** Meaning, everyone buys their own microphone and mic stand, and the rest of the PA system is purchased with money pooled from individual band members. (Or, they bring whatever they already have. Of course, this is going to work only with a component system.) Quint has done this in groups before. He was responsible for the mixer and the power amp, while the rest of the band took care of the speakers, other outboard gear, etc. When he moved from the area, there were no problems; he took his gear. The new band member who took Quint's place was responsible for bringing in gear to fill the void.

**2. Pay the owner a rental fee.** If one player already owns or goes ahead and buys a PA system, then the band should pay that individual some type of discounted gig rental fee. We'll leave it to you to figure out what is fair, but if you are the owner you should expect to be paid something. And if you're a non-owner, then you should expect to pay something.

**3. Buy band gear.** Beyond your PA system, this is the approach you should take for other band gear that can't be split up, such as vehicles, trailers, and lighting systems. Prior to the purchase, you need to create a written agreement that when the band purchases equipment together, a band member who leaves the band—for whatever reason—will be paid fair market value for his or her share of the gear. Now, this creates a problem for the player coming in, especially if they are poor, starting-musician types. After a number of years a player's share of band-owned gear—PA, lighting, band truck, etc.—can add up to a significant amount of money. So in your written agreement you may want to figure out a way to buy out the departing player over a longer period of time—six months to a year, perhaps.

Another long-term approach to buying band-owned gear is to decide on a certain percentage of every gig that will be taken out for band expenses. This allows the band to save for hard times when a major equipment problem or breakdown occurs. It's no fun when the PA breaks down and you have to devote the revenue from several gigs to repair or replace the thing. But saving $20 a gig can add up pretty fast. You'd be surprised. This plan also works well to finish paying off band gear that has been purchased on credit.

Any one of these three plans will work, as long as you think ahead and come up with some type of strategy for when the band breaks up. For some, buying band gear with other irresponsible musician-types is a very scary thought. But for others, it's just fine. Do what you feel is most comfortable. But do something.

## Firing someone

There's nothing more rewarding than finding the band member you need to complete your group. But there's a very real possibility that you may have to give these new friends and colleagues the pink slip somewhere down the road.

Nobody likes to fire a band member, yet it's sometimes essential for a band's growth. It can be messy as well as difficult: Every serious gigger has nightmare stories about the effects unit or mixer that mysteriously disappears after someone is fired from the band. A combination of good business savvy, as outlined above, and tactful manner will go a long way toward avoiding these nightmares.

The following section, taken from an article by Kenny Kerner, profiles a few bandleaders who were forced to fire musicians for various reasons. We've chosen to deal with each incident separately, so you can see what led up to this decision in each case, and then follow with a brief critique of how they handled the situation. Each situation was unique, yet in every instance the leader who did the firing: 1) had a really hard time doing it; 2) would do it all over again; and 3) feels the band is better off after the firing.

What follows are the stories of musicians taking care of business—even if it meant hurting a friend by telling him he's no longer in their band. In every case, the person who did the firing is also telling the story.

■ ■ ■

Modern Peasants
**Music style:** AAA
**Member fired:** violinist (March, 1998)
**Years in band:** 2
**Reasons for firing:** insubordination, lack of commitment
**Fired by:** Chuck Schiele
**Scenario:** "She was fine when we started, but as time went on she became more demanding and less available to us. She wanted to control all the money and wanted me to write all of her parts. She also didn't want to rehearse and only wanted to perform on shows that she felt were worthy of her time. She also had kind of a stuck-up attitude.

"We pretty much had a blowout over a few issues, mainly issues of insubordination—just BS, as far as I'm concerned. There's a time when you have to say that this player's BS is exceeding her talents and her contributions, and at that point I told the band that I'll be letting her go. As a matter of fact, I never really had the opportunity to personally tell her because she wouldn't respond to any of my phone calls. She ran into our bass player at a show and they spoke. During that conversation it got pretty dirty, and that's when she found out that we replaced her with another violinist and were having a ball without her."

**Critique:** As bandleader, Schiele made a decision and stuck to it. That's good. But having the fired player find out from another band member at someone else's show is not cool. You should always do a firing in person, not by email or on an answering machine. But if the person in question won't get on the phone, you may have no other choice. Just make sure they are told as soon as possible.

Little People
**Music style:** Top 40
**Members fired:** bassist, guitarist
**Reasons for firing:** irresponsibility, lack of talent
**Fired by:** T. C. Johnston
**Scenario:** "These were members of the band that we paid a salary so we didn't have to give them a piece of the band. One guy had a drinking problem and another played with us for only one day and we fired him for lack of talent. We were playing at a hotel on an Indian reservation in Wisconsin. It was a weekly gig that we had. This bass player started acting like a real freak by saying that he was gonna quit the band. We just told him to get outta there. But he decided he'd try to take a bunch of equipment with him, and we tried to stop him and ended up calling the police. Now our five-piece band was down to a four-piece band! I stayed up all night sequencing all the bass parts so we could play without a bassist.

"Within the next two days our guitarist exposes himself to a maid on reservation territory. The hotel manager was ready to fire the entire band for that—not to mention how angry the rest of the Native Americans were because the maid was also Indian. To smooth things over, I told the manager that we were disgusted with our guitar player's actions, and we fired him from the band. Our agent sent us a new guitarist and he couldn't play a lick, so we turned his amp way down and played as a three-piece with a sequencer that show. We later found out that the police were also looking for this guitarist because of an earlier incident. We finished up our last week of gigs and told all of the hired players that *we quit*. My partner and I packed up and moved to Vegas."
**Critique:** These guys obviously had it coming, and the bandleader was right in firing them. But telling hired players that the leaders were quitting was less than totally honest. It's right up there with telling an unwanted band member that "the band is breaking up" when it is

really going on without the fired member. Again, firing someone is uncomfortable but it goes with the job. Be honest about it.

The Rudies
**Music style:** ska
**Members fired:** vocalist, guitarist, trumpeter, drummer
**Years in band:** 2
**Reasons for firing:** lack of commitment and talent
**Fired by:** Tom Voris
**Scenario:** "We had a lot of people in the band at the time. All in all, we wound up letting five different players go for various reasons. We had a female backup singer whom we wanted to fire. So we let her sing one lead vocal and instead of firing her for lack of talent, we just took away that one lead song that she did and she quit. We just frustrated her into leaving the band, but it was done deliberately. The next person was the guitar player, who was always screwing around. We were all tight and we found it hard to come right out and say, 'You're fired.' The trumpet player was fired because of a lack of commitment; he just wasn't practicing. Nobody really liked him anyway, so we fired him. The next one to get fired was our drummer, who had difficulty keeping time. That was the hardest one 'cause everyone liked him."
**Critique:** Trying to frustrate someone into quitting is probably the worst way to "fire" anyone—a lesson Voris learned the hard way. "The backup singer tried to get even with me by starting a rumor that we were having an affair," he said. "The drummer was very upset but he understood the decision. I learned that the best way to fire someone is to just come right out and tell them to their faces. Always be up front with the band members."

Terminal Romance
**Music style:** alternative pop
**Members fired:** drummer, guitarist
**Years in band:** 2-3
**Reasons for firing:** drug abuse, different goals
**Fired by:** Dennis Barela
**Scenario:** "I was aware that the drummer was doing drugs for a while and noticed that it was getting progressively worse. He'd be out of breath just trying to keep up with certain songs. He'd show up late

and forget lots of things. We had a band meeting and talked about all the things we would have to go through—taking out ads and auditioning new members. It was a unanimous band decision to fire him. I gave him a phone call and told him over the phone, but he still managed to track me down at a friend's house that night. He called me outside and I thought he wanted to talk about it but instead he punched me in the mouth while he was high.

"The guitarist had also been in the band a few years when we had to fire him. He didn't really care for our type of music—he did it for the fun. He'd get there and pop open beers and start to party. We had another band meeting to discuss firing the guitarist and again it was unanimous. I called and let him know that our goals differed and maybe we should just go separate musical ways."

**Critique:** Barela handled his situation with class and in many ways better than any of our other examples. The result? He got punched in the mouth. "No regrets about either situation. In fact, the guitarist and I are still friends. You have to be honest and you must act immediately if there is a conflict. You can't waste time."

We know some bandleaders will put a member on probation of some kind before actually firing them. This sounds fair, and we have actually tried it ourselves in the past. However, our experience has been that it almost never solves the problem and that we end up firing the person anyway. Sometimes it's just best to go with your gut.

■ ▧ ▨

### Firing a Band Member: Do's and Don'ts

**1. Don't let a bad situation continue indefinitely.** When a band member continually messes up, always warn him or her that this kind of attitude and conduct cannot continue.

**2. Document each charge against the player by writing it down.** Note the date, time, and circumstance of the event. Otherwise, it's your word against theirs. It's always wise to present cold, hard facts.

**3. If your band member has a drug- or alcohol-related problem, don't bother with warnings.** Until and unless this player cleans up his or her act, firing is inevitable. Get it over with quickly.

**4. Always fire somebody in person—face to face.** Never leave a termination notice on an answering machine or via email. Do it professionally. Review the situation, read the charges from your notes, remind the member that you've cautioned them several times. Be firm and decisive. This is not a game.

**5. Don't leave anyone hanging.** Although many believe it's a lot easier to keep the player who is messing up while searching out a replacement, we feel the opposite. Cut them loose now and pay the price. If that price means using subs for three months while you find a new member, so be it. The last thing you want to do is keep carrying old baggage with you. It can be very destructive.

### What's in your name?

One thing we didn't get into earlier when we discussed marketing and band names is the question of ownership. And this is another legal issue that you may want to consider. If this is *your* band, and *you* started it, had the concept, etc., it would be wise for you to actually own the name. In the previous chapter we talked a bit about getting a DBA ("doing business as") license so you could have a band bank account. Filing for a DBA will also go a long way toward proving any claim you have on a name. Applying for a business license with your state or county tax authority will also give you some backup here.

The subject of trademark is just too complex to get into here, but it is one that can really screw things up. Take, for example, the case of the pioneering Texas jam band Little Sister. They had a large and loyal following, great gigs, and a substantial degree of success— including two CDs of their own material, one of which was released by a major label. After years of work, as they were ready to sign their second record contract, they were informed that there were at least a half dozen other bands in the U.S. working under the name Little Sister. One of those was a successful cover band that had taken care of business and could prove that it had been using the name first. The Texans were forced to change their name.

The fact is that the person or group who is working under a name first—*and who can prove it*—has the rights to the name. Period.

By now you should have a name, players, songs, a marketing plan, and a good idea how this totally crazed business works. It's time to talk gear and take care of the final technical preparations for doing a gig.

# Tech

**TECH 1**

## YOUR GEAR

*One thing that drives me nuts about working with newbies—especially onstage, and under the gun—is that they often don't know their own rigs. They haven't checked all their cables (if they even brought enough to begin with), they haven't checked their batteries, they haven't brought any extension cords, mics, carpets, or whatever they'll need because they really just don't know what they need, and I guess they half expect someone else to provide it for them.*

Gregory Morris

As the quote that leads this chapter attests, your personal gear can be a very big issue when you are ready to start gigging. Once you move from rehearsals to paying gigs, the sound quality and reliability go from being pretty important to downright crucial.

Instruments are literally tools of your trade. Gear must be road-worthy—even if you're only traveling half a mile to the local pub. But gear—especially instruments—is personal as well as practical. Furthermore, it does little good for us to tell you about totally pro stuff that costs way more than you can afford at this point in your gigging life. We can, however, give you some tips on what to look for and what separates pro gear from wannabe gear. We can also give you some tips on getting the most for your money. Finally, we will help you put together a good gig bag with everything you need for gigs and emergencies based on the instrument you play.

### What makes gear "pro"

One thing that novice giggers have going for them is that the general quality of musical gear has improved by quantum leaps in the past decade or so. We are at a point where even many inexpensive imported instruments are of pretty decent quality—at least good enough for your first gigs. When we get into sound systems in the next chapter, you'll see that there are some very specific ways to tell what "pro" gear is, but this is not as cut and dried when it comes to your personal gear. No matter how "pro" your rig is, though, the qualities you want from it are pretty universal—sturdiness, reliability, flexibility, and sound quality appropriate to the style of music you play. Let's look at some gigging "musts" for a few basic gigging instruments.

### Guitar and bass

Guitarists and bass players need to look at four areas of equipment: instruments, amps, effects, and accessories. Let's start with the instrument. This is an incredibly subjective area; the choice of instrument will be based as much on the style of music you are playing as on personal preferences—although the "obvious" choice is not always as obvious as you might think. Jazz guitarist Ted Greene has been seen many times playing a Tele, which most of us think of as a rock and especially country guitar, while rocker Ted Nugent has long favored a Gibson Byrdland, which is a stone jazz guitar. But, again, there are a few universal concerns:

Does it stay and play in tune? Is it fully shielded against extraneous noise? Are the pickups quiet when the guitar is not being played, or do they hum and buzz and go microphonic? Is the instrument capable of producing a range of versatile tones? Remember, you will be covering parts played by lots of different guitarists, and recreating a similar tone is a big part of your job. Finally, does the instrument have a pro look? Especially when you are starting out, many fellow players and even bookers will pass judgment based on whether you look like a pro before they ever hear you, and your gear is part of that pro look.

### Amps

Size and weight are big issues. Remember the Gigger's Law of Physics: The amp that weighs 40 pounds loading in to the gig weighs

140 loading out. Next, does it sound good at low volume? This is crucial and a reason why so many cover players have given up on classic tube amps that sound great loud but thin and wimpy at lower volumes. It's also a reason why you see so many guitarists with digital modeling amps onstage. Don't get us wrong: Tube amps sound great. It's just that we find modeling amps more versatile and easier to deal with when it comes to volume. Bill has used one exclusively for the past four years largely because it can give him the sound of a tube amp running full bore at a much lower volume. On a similar note, any gigging amp just about has to have presets or channel switching in order to cover a range of tones quickly. Finally, good-sounding direct outs for running that amp straight into the house PA are a definite consideration, especially for bass players.

## Effects

The biggest issue with effects is usually noise. Does that stomp box sound like a jet plane taking off when you plug it in? If so, pass and go for the quieter (and usually more expensive) choice. Next is what we call the road-worthiness factor. One of the basic rules is that gear made from cheap plastic will fail on your most important gig when the agent you have been trying to get in with is in the audience. So pick up that effects box. Does it have some heft, or does it feel like it will shatter if you drop it (which you will do)? Is there a solid "click" when you engage the switch, or is it hard to tell if you have actually turned it on? Does it use batteries only, or can it take a wall-wart power supply? As much as we have traditionally hated these little black boxes, they can save you a ton of dough in burnt-out batteries. Finally, if the unit can switch patches via MIDI (Musical Instrument Digital Interface—more on this when we get to keyboards) you may be able to turn several units on or off at the same time with a single switch.

## Accessories

Picks: make sure you have many extras if you use them. Ditto a capo if you need one. (Bill uses a capo on just one song in his set and has bought three or four in the last year because he can never find the damn thing when he needs it.) Straps should be strong and easily adjustable, and strap-locks are a virtual must.

## Drums

Los Angeles-based drummer Jim Hollister offers several great tips for drummers. First off, "The days of the monster Peter Criss drum set are gone. You can get away with Ringo's set unless you're playing in a Van Halen or Rush tribute band. Even when money and space are not a consideration, you'll notice that pro drummers are using these less-is-more kits." So think quality, not quantity.

In terms of upgrading from a novice kit (the one your mom bought you when you were 14), you don't have to do it all at once. "You can make an inferior set sound a lot better with good drum heads and quality cymbals," says Hollister. "You can't fake the cymbals." So put your money there, and into a new snare drum. You can upgrade piece by piece from there. Cymbals and a snare can be used with any set.

Retail stores will negotiate, explains Hollister. Look at floor models and be willing to wait for one to become available. "Shells are the number one things. Every company has its different series based on whether the drums are hand-crafted and the type of wood." The better shells are thinner, which make them less durable, which means you need more protection on the road. Hollister is very impressed with some of the smaller "gig kits" now available. "All the hardware stores in the seat, and the shells store inside the bass drum. That and your cymbal bag, and you'll be set." You can literally walk in the door of the club and be ready for sound check in ten minutes. (Which leaves plenty of time for drummer to set up the PA!)

## Keys

The kind of music you are playing and your role in the band will play a big part in your choices here. If you are doing dance-pop, your needs will weigh heavily toward samplers, sequencers, and sound modules, with perhaps a single keyboard controller. Classic rock, jazz, or country will lean heavily on basic sounds like piano, organ, and strings. Those choices are beyond the scope of this book but, again, there are some universal basics.

As always, size and weight are a big concern. The good news is that even full-size 88-key keyboards are available in forms that will fit in a compact car and won't break your back.

For basic gigging, look for a board that can handle a range of basic sounds. Another major consideration is navigation, or getting quickly and easily from one sound to another. In the heat of battle that is a live gig, you don't have time to wander through dozens of buttons or submenus to get to a basic piano/strings layer.

Make sure the board is built solid. Most of the home keyboards on the market sound pretty good but are not made to be moved around a lot. Also, less-than-pro boards will almost always use a wall-wart AC adapter to provide power. While "off-board" power supplies are pretty common, the "lump on a rope" variety is easier to plug into a standard power strip and less likely to fail. Here are photos of both types so you know the difference.

**"Off-board" power supply**          **"Lump on a rope" power supply**

Finally, connections are important. Almost all keyboards on the market today are stereo, but it is important that your selection has a mono output, too, and the sounds must "translate" well to mono because many of the systems you will be playing through will not be capable of stereo operation.

Also, make sure to check for MIDI connections. Most all keyboards made in the past 15 years are MIDI-capable, allowing you to control other keyboards or sound modules from your board via the MIDI out or access your onboard sounds with another keyboard via the MIDI in. It also allows you to switch presets or programs on multiple units from one master switch, as well as to control sequencers and loops.

## Singers

This one is pretty simple. Own a mic. Own a cable. Own a stand. While you're at it, buy a monitor and seriously consider owning your own PA system (at least a practice system). The fact that your instrument is built into your body does not let you off the hook when it comes to gear.

## Cables

Before we get out of the area of personal gear, let's talk just a bit about cables. This is an area where it is easy—and exceedingly stupid—to skimp. A cable may not look cool or be sexy or even seem like that big a deal. But consider this: All of that sound that you have so diligently worked out in rehearsal and painstakingly finessed through hours on end of personal practice gets to the audience via those lengths of wire. If a cable fails or just cuts in and out or crackles, then all that work was for naught because the audience will only hear the noise or, worse, hear nothing at all.

It comes down to this: Buy the best cable you can afford. The one that came in the box with your guitar or bass or keyboard is likely of low quality; your best bet is to just throw it in the trash right away. Look for high-quality connectors like Neutrik or Switchcraft, and good cable like Canare or Belden. This goes for each and every cable you use, including mic and instrument, MIDI, every single cable in your PA rack if you have one, and even your speaker cables.

## Getting your money's worth

Gigging musicians are almost always on the lookout to either replace or upgrade some instrument or piece of gear. You either want to sound better, look better—or think you are playing better. While spending money doesn't always equate to playing better, it does make a difference. A couple of years ago Quint upgraded from mid-line acoustic guitar to a $1,000-plus acoustic and was amazed at how much better he began playing, both technically and emotionally.

But with so much invested in gear, how will you ever actually make any money? For most pros and many semi-professional musicians, the bulk of what they earn gets reinvested in gear. Whatever your situation, you have to know how and when to buy your gear. The last thing you want to be doing is walking into a local store and paying full retail. Here are a few tips to help you get the most for your money when buying instruments or equipment.

**Used gear.** Before buying a brand new piece of gear, ask yourself if it really has to be new to get the job done. Many older instruments are of a higher quality than newer instruments. (For this reason, they are often more expensive too.) But this is not always the case, especially for accessories and things like that. Check local newspapers, music papers, music store bulletin boards, and Internet sites like eBay for what you need. If you can't find it—or a functional equivalent—then you'll have to buy new. (Keep in mind that many new items are offered on Internet auction sites.)

**Support your local retailer.** All these megastores and Web sites provide great prices, but they don't always do much to support the local music scene. They can't always provide you personal service and advice either. During the past decade, literally thousands of local musical instrument retailers have gone out of business due to increasing competition from superstores and Web sites. Local music stores play an important part in the health of your local music scene, so if it's just a matter of saving a few dollars, support your local store. Granted, it's not your duty to keep that local music store in business, but they can't survive selling you a dozen picks and a set of strings every month. Furthermore, because they know they aren't the only game in town anymore, they are more open than ever to negotiating on price.

**Research and more research.** Whether or not you end up buying at your local retailer, you need to start off by doing as much research as possible. Once you've decided on the instrument or piece of gear you need, or at least narrowed it down to several models, while checking out the deals at local stores, get on the Web as well and start looking for the best prices. In addition to Ebay, a few of the major retailer Web sites include Musicians Friend, Mars Music, American Musical Supply, and Sweetwater, but there are many more. While you are at these sites, you should also sign up for their snail mail catalogs. (Don't sign up for any email lists. They can be very annoying when you're not in a buying mode.) Be sure and check out scratch and dents, closeouts, and special Internet offer sections on these Web sites. (For links to websites, go to www.covergigs.com.)

Once you've found the best price, you need to decide if that retailer or mail order house is worthy of your business. Have they been in business for years, or might they be a fly-by-night operation? Many smaller retailers sell new gear on eBay. Just be sure to read their seller ratings: What is the ratio of satisfied to unsatisfied customers?

There should be very few, if any, dissatisfied customers. Also check out their return policy, and look for special "no interest or payments for 90 days" offers and the like. These are excellent "money stretching" techniques, as long as you pay them off in time. If you don't, you'll get stuck in the rut of 20 percent credit card interest payments, which can take years to pay off. So only use credit cards if you know you are going to pay them off quickly! Also, keep in mind that you won't be paying any sales tax if you are buying from a retailer outside your state. This can really ad up on big-ticket items.

**Negotiate locally.** Before you buy online, take that price and see if you can negotiate a similar price at local stores. In addition to supporting the local retailer you'll also be able to get your hands on your gear immediately, which is half the fun when you have "got to have it" fever. Just simply say that you found Model X on the Web for $X and were wondering if they could match or beat this price. Just be straightforward and matter-of-fact about it. While you will have to pay sales tax, you won't have to pay any shipping, which can add up for weightier items. If they can come close, then you should buy it locally; if not, then go back to the Web or the mail-order house. But keep in mind that in the long run there is a lot more to buying a piece of gear than getting the best price.

Negotiating can work for national retailers as well. Quint recently bought a piece of recording gear and saved about $100 by bringing in a printout of a Web page that showed a better price from a smaller competitor.

One thing you will find offered on virtually every piece of gear you buy is the extended warranty. About all we can tell you is that neither of us ever buy them. If you buy good quality gear in the first place, it comes with a good warranty and that should be sufficient. However, extended warranties are good for two things: 1) If a piece of gear fails under an extended warranty, you can generally walk into the store and walk out with a replacement instead of waiting around for a repair. If you are gigging a lot this can be a big deal. 2) With higher-tech gear, an extended warranty can be looked at as "technology insurance." If the piece fails and has to be replaced, you will almost surely get the latest model, which may have more features and better sound than your original.

## Making it roadworthy

It would definitely be cool to start your gigging days off with black, hard-shell flight cases for all your gear—complete with your band name stenciled in white on every surface. But let's face reality; that may not happen until you hit The Big Time. It's going to take most of your money to get the actual gear, let alone cases to provide perfect protection. Until then, you'll have to get by with a little money and a lot of ingenuity.

You can start off by using the box that any particular piece of gear came in. That includes the pretty, point-of-purchase box that you saw in the store, but in many cases (pardon the pun) it also includes the plain brown box the unit was shipped to the store in. Coming from the manufacturers, these boxes are set up to take a good beating. If you order via a catalog or the Internet, you will get both boxes, so you're all set. These won't last you forever, but depending on the number of gigs you do and how you pack your gear, they may last quite a while. One thing that's great about these boxes is that they are very square or rectangular, no weird shapes, which is great for packing. Granted, they don't look that cool, but they get the job done.

If you have too much pride to use the original boxes, and you have a little money, then you can try the "another man's junk is your road case" plan. We're talking wooden crates, ammo boxes, foot lockers, old and odd suitcases—the kinds of things you find at surplus and second-hand stores. If you have a large college or university in your area, call and ask if they have a surplus shop; you may stumble across great finds there as well. After finding the right box, you will also need to buy some Styrofoam or foam rubber and cut it to the shape of the gear with an X-acto knife or razor blade.

Up from this level is buying soft-shell, foam/canvas-type, or semi-hard-shell cases. These look good, but aren't made for the rigors of the road, though they will work for band members who travel short distances in separate cars. But once you start loading things in the back of a truck or van, be sure to keep these types of cases on top. Don't spend half the money for half the protection, because half the protection still gets your gear damaged. If you're going to buy "real" cases, your ultimate goal should be hard-shell, ATA-approved flight cases. ATA stands for Airline Transportation Association and represents this organization's "seal of approval" as the highest level of protection for transporting equipment. Oh, and don't forget spray paint your or your band's name across the cases to look profoundly professional. (Just be sure to use a stencil.)

Along with this collection of cases should come several dollies, hand trucks, or carts. Trash-can dollies will do. Flexible shipping straps can also help secure boxes and cases and keep things from falling when you're transporting gear from the truck to the stage.

## Gig bags

> *Encourage novice giggers to set their rigs up—start to finish—in several rooms of their house/school/whatever so that they can anticipate problems before they get to the stage or even rehearsals. Remind them that most stages don't have electrical outlets everywhere and that often you'll need to set up far away from your amp (need long guitar cables as well as short) and/or your amp will need an extension cord. Drummers will need their own mats/rugs to prevent kick-drum creeping; bass and keys should have their own D.I. boxes and patch cables; vocalists should travel with their own mics.*

This quote, from the same gigger who started us out on this chapter, is a good lead-in to all of the stuff you might not think about until you get to the gig and find that you... *need it now!* This is why we have *gig bags*.

By "gig bag" we don't mean the soft sort-of cases that many giggers use to transport their instruments on the gig. In fact, it does not even have to be a bag. Bill's is a hideously bright yellow plastic toolbox, while Quint favors an old Samsonite suitcase. Here is a list of what should be in that bag—both the basics and some specific items for your instrument.

## The basics

Duct tape or gaffers tape (gaffers tape is much better as it does not leave the disgusting, sticky residue that duct tape does when you remove it, but it is harder to find and fairly expensive), a basic tool kit (screwdrivers, a crescent wrench, pliers, wire cutters, scissors,

Allen wrenches, maybe a soldering iron), batteries in every size your gear uses, spare cables, fuses (for your amp), spare cables (mic, ¼", MIDI, long, short—basically backups of whatever you normally use), AC extension cords, and power strips.

Guitarists should add picks, strings, a towel to wipe down your instrument and keep the grunge off, a quick string winder, an extra strap, and a tuner.

Bassists should add all of that with the exception of picks if you don't use them. They should also carry a direct box if their amp does not have direct outs.

Keyboard players should add ... one word—backups. If you do not carry some kind of backup of sound patch data for your synths and safety versions of any sequences and/or samples you use, rest assured that at some point something will fail and you will be stuck with a pretty keyboard that does not make any sounds—or at least not the ones you need it to make.

Drummers need extra sticks, a second kick pedal (or at least springs and the leather strap if you use a belt drive rather than a chain), tuning keys, extra snare (drum or actual snare springs plus snare cord or plastic strips), pair of snare heads (especially the bottom head), kick head, and cymbal nuts.

Singers (and by this we mean anyone who sings, not just dedicated lead vocalists) should add throat lozenges or Chloroseptic, and their own mic. Yes, the venue will sometimes provide a mic, and some sound techs will even insist that you use a specific model that they provide because they know how that mic sounds through the house system. Regardless, you should own and carry your own mic. You will use it more often than not.

With your personal gear taken care of, lets take a quick detour into Rehearsal Land before we hit the stage and count down to that first song.

# TECH 2

# REHEARSAL SPACE, GEAR, AND RECORDING

*Rehearsal time is not gear repair time. Find a place that you can leave the gear set up so you don't spend all your rehearsal time being roadies. Be aware of the neighbors— Marshalls on 11 aren't necessary, and if you can play a song quietly then you really know you can actually play it! Always record the rehearsal to catch flubs and settle disputes about who's playing what.*

Tom Skidmore

Any true performing musician longs for the stage, longs to play live in front of a crowd. But you'll actually be spending more time in the rehearsal studio than just about anywhere else. And while we have already discussed the basics of how and how often to rehearse, there are some technical and equipment issues that we've saved for this section of the book.

Having a rehearsal space of your own, someplace where you can leave as much equipment set up as possible, will save you a lot of time and go a long way toward helping your band progress. Setting up and tearing down every practice in your (or your parent's) family room is no fun. (It probably won't thrill your housemates or family either.)

In this chapter we will take a look at how to choose rehearsal space and get it at least somewhat soundproofed. Then we'll look at rehearsal gear. Finally, we'll examine the one thing you can do at a rehearsal that will do more for your band's sound than just about anything else: Record it.

## Setting up a rehearsal space

With the right combination of material, ingenuity, and sweat, you can turn just about any large room into a reasonably soundproof rehearsal space. By "soundproofing" we mean keeping the sound generated inside a space from getting outside; this is different from acoustically treating a space intended for critical studio recording. This isn't as hard as it seems; in fact, we know of one player who put a studio in a mobile home and went for years without a complaint, despite the fact that the neighbors were a mere six feet away.

Here are a few tips to help you follow your muse and keep peace in the neighborhood. You will notice that all of our sources asked to remain anonymous. This is due to regulations in many cities that forbid the use of living space for any other purpose. Be sure to check the laws in your area before *quietly* proceeding.

## Choosing a space

First, take stock of what you need. How big is your band? A six-piece obviously needs more space than a power trio, but beyond that, make sure that you're not too crowded. Tempers tend to heat up in confined quarters, especially as the temperature rises. (And a group of musicians playing with passion in an unventilated, small space can get steamy pretty fast.)

Do you live in a semi-rural or a densely populated area? Your location dictates how much you have to spend on construction and equipment. How much you play and how often you'll be using the space will also factor into the mix. After all, there's no point in shelling out thousands of bucks for room treatments if you only get together a couple of Saturday afternoons a month.

Let's assume that you live in an urban area and you rehearse once or twice a week. We'll also assume your name isn't Rockefeller and you'll be doing the room makeover yourself.

If you are lucky enough to live in a place with a basement, then you're already halfway there. If you are in a basement, your biggest worry is how to keep sound out of the house above. Many of the techniques that follow will apply in basement setups, but you lucky subterraneans will just have to worry about a single surface instead of four like the rest of us.

## Take it from the top

First, a drop-acoustic ceiling helps. It's not going to hermetically seal in the sound, but it will definitely take a bite out of it. Bill installed acoustic tile and frame in a  20'x20' garage for a couple hundred bucks. Also, while commercial-grade acoustic tile works okay, there are tiles on the market that fit into a standard drop-ceiling frame and are designed specifically for soundproofing. These work pretty well, but they are substantially more expensive.

Wall treatments have triggered spirited debates over what works best. Our advice? Forget carpeting. Sure, you can pick up carpet scraps dirt-cheap or free. The problem is, they deaden the sound inside the room while doing virtually nothing to keep it from leaking out. There are, however, several soundproofing products that really work, are easy to install, and are priced so that you don't have to mortgage your first-born. Companies like Auralex and Markertek make sound-absorbent foam panels in various sizes; these are worth checking out if you don't want to get into a big construction job. Auralex also offers a publication called *Acoustics 101* free of charge on its Web site to aid the novice soundproofer. Point your browser to http://www.auralex.com.

If you really want to get serious about soundproofing and you've got the bucks, consider some tips from a Southern California-based musician who has put together a very nice space.

Starting from the bottom up, our expert covered the floor with *sound board* (a drywall-like board designed to absorb sound; it should be available at your favorite building supply store). The procedure works whether you're carpeting or installing hardwood on the floor surface. It's necessary because the vibrations from the band—especially low-end villains like bass and drums—will carry down the sidewalk, around the corner, and up the neighbors' driveway right into their house, regardless of what you do to the walls and ceiling. "That's something that most people miss when they're building their studio," he says. "They just think, If I put down carpet that'll be the end of it, but that doesn't always do it."

If you're building the studio in a garage, you're probably going to have an exterior wall with studs on the inside. Our contact installed sound board between the studs, added insulation, then built a sandwich-type wall alternating sound board and dry wall for a total of four layers. How thick you make the sandwich depends on what your wallet can handle and what you think your neighbors will put up with. Remember to configure the door the same way.

Once the ceiling was stuffed with 12-inch-thick scrap foam rubber picked up for a song from a furniture upholsterer, the room was essentially isolated. The result is a room with bare walls, which gives the musicians a more natural sound.

Naturally, for a setup like this, it helps if you're handy with tools. Otherwise, you're going to be paying to put some contractor's kid through college.

Our contact also noted that the best soundproofing tip is to make friends with your neighbors. Give them your phone number, so that if the sound cranks up above their pain threshold, they can call you rather than somebody wearing blue!

## Headphone rehearsals

So you can't afford to dedicate a room to your rehearsal needs? Check it out: You can rehearse an entire rock band in an apartment or your living room, thanks to things like electronic drums and multichannel headphone amps—possibly the greatest peacekeeping devices between you and your neighbors since the invention of walls.

Samson, Rane, Rolls, Furman, and a bunch of other companies make rack-mountable headphone amps that will run anywhere from four to a dozen sets of cans, each with its own volume control.

Years ago, Quint's band negotiated to rent a small, two-room office in a two-story office building. The main point in the contract was that the band was not allowed to "make any noise" before 7 p.m. weekday nights. (By then the normal office types were out of the building.) The band used the small reception room for the drummer and put the lead guitarist's amp in a closet off the main room. These were miked, while the rest of the band plugged directly into the mixer. Everyone wore headphones for recording-studio style rehearsals.

There are some disadvantages to this approach. For one, the drummer generally has to use electronic drums—though not always, as in Quint's example. Then, too, there is headphone fatigue. They can get hot, bulky, and tiresome on your sweaty ears after a full session.

But those might be small prices to pay to keep from getting evicted.

## Rehearsal gear

Having to set up gear for rehearsals is a drag and can massively cut into the time you have to actually rehearse. In order to deal with this inconvenience, players often start leaving personal gear set up in the common rehearsal room; while this does cut into personal practice time at home, it does save time and spare some physical effort when it comes to rehearsal. Having to set up and tear down all the time is why so many bands rehearse at the drummer's house. Yes, drummers are screwed unless they own a second set they can leave at the rehearsal space or the session is at their place to begin with. For everyone else, there are options.

Guitarists (especially volume freaks who play half-stacks) should seriously consider getting their hands on something smaller to use for rehearsals. Make sure your stomp boxes are on a pedal board and can be set up in two minutes or less (great gig advice as well). Same goes for rack rigs: Keep 'em pre-wired and not setup-challenged. Bassists should look at a good amp simulator or direct box and run it through the PA. Make it as easy on yourself as you can without sacrificing too much on the tonal side. Same goes for keyboard players.

Just as individual band members need to scale down their gear for rehearsals, the same goes for their PA systems. You don't *need* a full PA system for rehearsals, nor do you want to hassle with setting it up. Your main PA system may make you sound or feel better, but it's not worth the time and effort required to set up and break down just for practice.

As mentioned above, your first option is headphone rehearsals. The advantage is all you have to set up is the mixer. The disadvantage is electronic drums and/or blown-out ears. The second option is to purchase a small rehearsal PA. Solo PA systems with four inputs and reverb have really come down in price in recent years and may be worth the investment. You might also consider using parts of your main system. For example, you could buy a basic powered mixer and then use your stage monitors as the mains in your rehearsal studio. Keep this in mind as you put together your onstage monitoring system—it may also double as a rehearsal PA system.

Here's another option to avoid all PA and soundproofing problems: Go acoustic. Rehearse with acoustic guitars, bass, and a practice pad or conga drum for the drummer. Keyboard players can use a small practice amp, or they might have a consumer-oriented keyboard with built-in speakers. The bottom line through all this is that practices don't have to be loud—they just have to be good. Individual members can dial up the right "sounds" on their own; band practice is about learning *together* and getting tight.

Finally, the issue of rehearsal gear applies even if you are renting time in a rehearsal studio—it takes time from actual rehearsal, and the more gear that has to be moved and set up, the less enthusiastic folks will stay about rehearsing, or at least rehearsing regularly. Almost every rehearsal studio we know of provides a PA that is set up and ready to go. Some also provide a basic drum kit and some guitar and bass amps. While these places can be a little bit more expensive than the bare-bones operations, you should consider spending the extra bucks. Making rehearsal less of a hassle is always a good thing.

## Recording rehearsals

You may think you have an objective ear while you're practicing, but in reality you don't. You never sound as good (or bad!) as you think you do *while* you are listening to yourself play. This is why is it is wise to have a more objective set of ears at your rehearsal sessions: a recorder.

You don't have to record every song, and the recording setup does not have to be technically complex or expensive. Though both of us have recorded rehearsals, we decided to pass this subject off to someone who really knows how to do it. Bruce Bartlett, a senior mic engineer for Crown International, is responsible for several patents in the audio field. He has written a number of books on recording. If you want to really approach recording rehearsal the right way, then check out these bits of wisdom from Bruce:

Most bands I record are surprised that recording can be so educational. By listening to their recording, the band members can hear their performance very clearly. That helps them play better. As one musician told me, "We're playing a lot tighter since we recorded our CD."

A recording holds up a mirror to your performance. Is the group tight? Is the rhythm backup working? Is the arrangement too busy? The recording will tell you. It's easier to evaluate your performance when you're just listening to a recording of it, without playing your instrument. Then you can take steps to improve.

You don't have to record an album to get these benefits. Consider recording your band's practice sessions. The sound quality is not critical. You mainly want to evaluate your performance, and that's possible as long as you can hear everyone in the mix.

Most important, you can record your rehearsals with simple methods, so the technology doesn't get in the way as you're playing. Once you settle on a way that works for you, it can become a standard part of your rehearsals.

### Simple recording

This is the easiest way to record, and it might work fine for you. Get a portable cassette recorder or boom box with a built-in microphone. In your practice room, walk around as the band is playing, and find a spot where you hear a good mix of the instruments and PA vocals. Put the recorder there, on a table, or on the floor—whatever gives the best-sounding recordings.

Many portable cassette recorders have an automatic record-level feature. If yours doesn't, set the record level so that the recorder's meter peaks as high as possible without going into the red. Listen to the playback. If it sounds distorted even though the recording level was correct, chances are that the built-in mic or the mic preamp in the recorder was overloaded by the loud volume of your band. Place the recorder farther away from the band, or play more quietly, and see if that solves the problem.

### Recording and a mic

A step up from a cassette recorder is a Minidisk, CD, or DAT recorder. Since they do not include a microphone, you'll need a separate mic that plugs into the recorder. If you're using a CD recorder, which does not have mic inputs, plug the mic into a mic preamp or small mixer to amplify the mic level up to the line level required by the CD recorder. Then plug the small mixer's output into the CD recorder's line input.

What kind of microphone should you use? Almost anything will do the job. You might try a PZM or two on the floor. Or use a pair of cardioid microphones on stands, facing toward the band and spread apart a few feet. The mic's cardioid polar pattern will reduce pickup of muddy-sounding room acoustics. Record in stereo if possible—compared to mono, stereo makes it easier to hear what each band member is playing because each instrument is separated in space in the stereo playback.

Check your recorder to see what kind of mic input connectors it has. If it uses a ¼" or ⅛" phone jack, you'll need to make an adapter cable. Figure 1 shows how to wire a balanced mic (with a 3-pin XLR-type connector) to a mono phone plug. Figure 2 shows how to connect two mics to a stereo phone plug. (Many Minidisk and portable DAT recorders use mini stereo phone plugs.) The left mic is wired to the mini plug tip; the right mic is wired to the mini plug ring, and the shields from both mics go to the mini plug sleeve.

If your recording mics are condenser types with XLR connectors, and they require phantom power, connect the mics to the phantom-power supply input. Connect the output of the supply to the adapter described above.

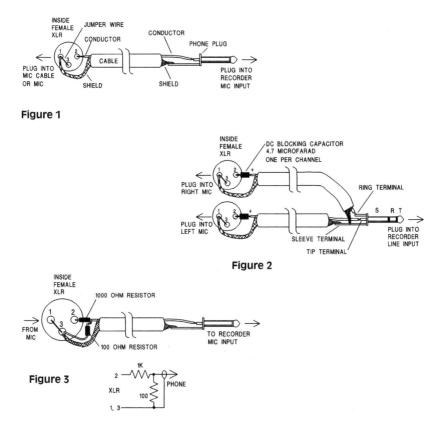

**Figure 1**

**Figure 2**

**Figure 3**

Note: Some recording mics are small condenser types with unbalanced outputs, powered by DC power (not phantom power) from a mic input. Mics that plug into a sound card, and receive power from the sound card, are that type. If that's the kind of mics you are using, omit the DC blocking capacitors shown in Figure 2. Otherwise the mics won't work.

Is the playback distorted? Probably the volume of your band is making the mic put out a really hot signal, which is overdriving the mic preamp in the recorder. A *pad* prevents this distortion. This is a two-resistor circuit (Figure 3) that is wired between your mics and the recorder mic inputs. The pad reduces the signal level coming from the mic so that it does not overload the mic preamp.

**Recording via your mixer**

A drawback of using one or two mics to record your band is that they pick up a lot of room acoustics, which can muddy the sound. You might prefer to record directly off your mixing board instead. If you mic all your instruments and vocals individually, and run the mic signals through the board, you'll record a clean signal without room acoustics.

Recording off the board is more complicated than recording with mics because you have to place several mics and set up a good mix. But once this is done, the recording process is simple.

You don't need elaborate drum miking to make practice tapes. Try one cardioid mic overhead and one in the kick. Or get a *mini omni* mic (a lavaliere mic like newscasters wear). Tape it to a 5" coat hanger wire, and tape the wire to the right side of the snare drum. The mic should be about 4" over the top rim. This single mic will pick up the entire kit.

Connecting to the mixing board is easy. Find a spare main output or two on your board, and connect it to your recorder line input(s), using a suitable cable. If your mixer has only one output that is connected to a power amp, plug a Y-cord into the output so that it will feed both the power amp and your recorder.

Now you're ready to record. Here's a step-by-step procedure:

1. Set your board's master faders at design center (the shaded part of fader travel).
2. As the band is playing a loud song, turn up each input-trim con-

trol until the clip light comes on, then turn down the input trim 6 to 10 dB to create some headroom. Repeat for each input channel.

3. Set up a rough mix while keeping the board's meters peaking around 0 maximum. You might try setting the mix while listening on headphones.

4. Record the mix and play back the tape.

5. If any instrument or vocal is too loud in the mix, turn it down a few dB on your mixer.

6. Repeat steps 4-5 until the recorded mix is okay.

Is the recording distorted? Maybe the mixer output is +4 dBu level, but your recorder input wants to see a –10 dBV signal. This is likely if the mixer output is a 3-pin XLR-type connector, and your recorder line input is a phone or phono jack. In that case, turn down the mixer master faders so that the mixer meters peak around –12 VU maximum. The recorder should be able to handle that level without distortion.

■ ■ ■

There you have some easy techniques to record practice tapes. By listening to the recordings, you can hear how your band performs, and then you can work out ways to play better. The other great benefit of recording rehearsals is you have a permanent record of both your own progress and your band's progress. Quint has band rehearsal recordings from 25 years ago; recently he transferred a few of the best songs from each band over the years to digital format. The result is an extended history of his musical adventures—which his kids love to listen to and laugh at!

## Heading to the stage

With all the tips you've found in this chapter, your band will be practicing comfortably and efficiently—without interruptions from the police or neighbors. As you record your rehearsals you'll also be recognizing your weaknesses and dealing with them. The goal is to get onstage. But before you can do so, you need to have a handle on what separates you from your audience and delivers your sound to them: your PA system. That's what we'll cover in the next chapter as we work through the technical issues involved in playing a gig.

# TECH 3

# PA BASICS

*I wish I had known many years ago how to run a sound system. The first time out, with all the excitement and everything else, it's easy to forget that the sound system is the main line to the crowd. Please take a little time to learn the basics of what makes your system tick. Then after a few years you will really appreciate the good sound companies you work with. Until then, be nice to them, since they can make or break you with a quick flip of one finger.*

R. Sanders

Now comes the part that most bands find hardest: learning how to set up and operate the PA. It is odd how so many potential giggers fall down at this point, because the truth is that if you can set up a guitar rig with a few stomp boxes and dial in a decent sound, then almost all of that knowledge transfers over to your PA system.

### The parts of a sound system

Before you drop a bunch of dough on a lot of audio gear, take some time to learn about the parts of a system, how they work together, and the basics of what each of those parts does. It will make things much easier in the long run.

No matter what kind of system you buy, there are five basic system parts you need to know about: mics, mixers, amps, speakers, and processors. The phrase "garbage in-garbage out," though coined by computer types, is the best rule we can think of when approaching audio, so let's begin at the beginning of the sound chain: microphones.

The mic world has gotten pretty interesting in the past couple of years, especially for first-band giggers. Not very long ago, giggers had just a couple of basic mic choices available to them. On one side were the pro, great-sounding industry standards that everyone in the audio biz used. Unfortunately, they tended to be a bit expensive. On the other side were the "Radio Shack Specials." But all that has changed. The past few years have brought a slew of budget-priced mics made by the same manufacturers with performance comparable to the higher-end stuff, but at prices even baby bands can afford.

## Vocal versus instrument mics

As you get started in the world of gigging sound, you will likely not be too worried about instrument mics, with the exception of a couple of good drum mics, or if you have horns in the band. But it's important to know the differences between a vocal mic and an instrument mic. Let's use a couple of classics as examples.

Without a doubt the most used vocal mic in the history of gigging is the workhorse Shure SM-58. This hand-held, dynamic cardioid mic (more on those terms in a minute) is reasonably priced, with a well-deserved reputation for durability. It also has something called a midrange presence "bump" that many other mics have duplicated over the years. This means that the SM-58 does not actually reproduce all frequencies equally. Instead, it gives a slight emphasis to frequencies in the 2kHz to 5kHz range, which makes the SM-58 sound particularly good for vocals (although female vocalists need to be very careful with these presence bumps, which can make them sound harsh).

Another version of that mic, the Shure SM-57, is more widely thought of as an "instrument" mic. The difference between the two? The SM-58 has a ball-shaped end made of steel mesh with a built-in foam layer inside known as a *windscreen* or *pop filter*. This piece of material helps cut down on "s" sounds which come off like a windstorm, and popping "p" sounds. The SM-57 does not have this filter. That being said, note that the SM-58 has been used as an instrument mic countless thousands of times, and the SM-57 is a popular choice among some vocalists.

## Directionality

Vocal microphones for giggers generally require some *directionality* so that the mic emphasizes the sounds in front of the windscreen and suppresses sounds coming from the sides or rear. The common types of mic directionality patterns are *omni-directional* (which picks up equally from all directions), *cardioid*, and *super- or hyper-cardioid*. A heart-shaped polar plot, known as a *cardioid plot* (from the word "cardio," meaning heart), will allow more sound to enter from the front of the mic than the sides or rear; a super- or hyper-cardioid pattern narrows the opening and further rejects sound coming from the sides. (Be aware that while super- and hyper-cardioid mics reject more side or "off-axis" sound, they actually allow more sound to enter the mic from the rear than their simple cardioid brethren. Keep this in mind when it comes time to place monitors.) The super-cardioid advantage of more off-axis suppression may be a disadvantage if the vocalist is too busy dancing all over the stage to stay in front of the mic (or just has bad mic technique), or if many vocalists are sharing the same mic.

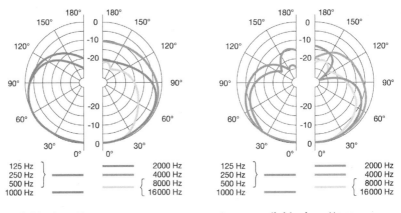

**Cardioid mic pattern**             **Super-cardioid mic pattern**

Cardioid-patterned microphones also tend to exhibit a proximity effect, in which the bass frequencies (50 to 200Hz) are emphasized when the singer's lips draw two inches or closer to the front part of the mic's windscreen. Different mics have varying amounts of proximity effect, depending on internal construction. Many artists use this effect as part of their vocal performance by "working the mic," drawing close for soft-voiced parts that take advantage of the bass response, then moving back to belt out a loud part with increased clarity.

## Microphone construction

Many types of mics are used in the studio for recording, but for gigging the most popular choices boil down to two: *dynamic* and *condenser*. Dynamic microphones resemble the common loudspeaker assembly, with a winding of wire (a voice coil) suspended on the vibrating element (cone or diaphragm) that's centered within a magnetic circuit. As sound pressure from the singer's voice moves the diaphragm, the coiled wire moves back and forth, disturbing the magnetic field and thus creating a proportional voltage in the coil. This voltage is usually sent to a matching transformer within the body of the microphone and on to the male XLR pins. Dynamic microphones require no other power source and are generally built rugged to withstand abuse and very high sound pressure levels.

Though used less frequently on gigs than dynamic microphones, condenser microphones offer a few advantages over their dynamic counterparts. The transducer element of a condenser mic uses the principle of varying capacitance, in which the plates of the capacitor (condenser) are the flexible diaphragm and an inflexible back plate. Since the diaphragm of a condenser mic does not contain a voice coil (as in dynamic mics), the condenser mic diaphragm can be made of very thin film materials that can respond accurately to sounds for increased clarity. The low mass of the diaphragm permits very exacting capture of transient sounds plus extended high-frequency response. The disadvantage for most professional condenser mics is the need for battery or phantom power sent from the mixer to the electronics in the mic that convert the variable capacitance output to a corresponding voltage output for the XLR connection.

## Other factors

Other factors that affect your choice of vocal microphone concern how you plan to use the mic during performance. Its weight may become an issue: Most dynamic mics are between 8 and 11 ounces, and if this is too much to handle all night, a condenser mic, which tends to be lighter, may be preferable.

Windscreens are another factor: A small windscreen will show off your facial expressions more, but a larger one or an additional foam windscreen may be needed if you work in windy environments.

Then there's the trend toward wireless microphones. Although much more expensive than wired mics, wireless systems that include a microphone and a high-quality transmitter are available at more modest prices every day. Today, a good wireless mic system (mic/transmitter and receiver) will set you back about $1,000, and professional quality from $1,000 to $4,000. Until wireless systems begin to challenge wired mics on a cost and performance basis, many giggers will opt to invest their precious few dollars on the mic element alone.

## Speakers

Because they are somewhat similar in nature, we are going to move from the first step of the process to the last step and take a look at speakers. (By "similar in nature" we mean that both mics and speakers are *transducers*—that is, they convert one form of energy to another. A mic converts acoustic energy or sound pressure into electrical energy, while a speaker converts electrical energy into acoustic energy.) For live gigging sound, you will be concerned with two types of speaker enclosures: mains and monitors.

## Mains

This is what the audience hears. Ideally, *all* the sound the audience hears should come from these speakers, but the reality of many if not most gigging bands is that the mains are typically used for vocals plus perhaps a bit of kick drum, plus maybe keys and horns if you have them. Why? Truth is that those of us who use amps as a part of our sound (that would be bassists and, primarily, guitarists) tend to play too loud, and in small to medium-size venues miking these amps is a waste of time unless you can get these players to turn down their stage rigs.

Historically, nearly all speaker enclosures were passive—that is, they needed to be fed with an amplified signal in order to operate. The trend more recently has been toward powered speaker cabinets, which include amps and sometimes other electronics onboard. These powered enclosures receive a "line level" signal from the mixer and handle the entire rest of the process of creating sound. Besides simplicity, the big advantage of these powered enclosures is that they tend to sound very good. Audio pros get paid well not so much for knowing how to set up and run systems as for more specialized knowledge like matching amps to speakers and knowing the little things that can make a system really sing. With all of the electronics built in and optimized for integrated use, you get some of the advantages of that knowledge without having to hire someone.

You will, however, pay for that advantage. Yes, the downside of powered enclosures is that they can be pricey. But when you look at the whole package and price out the individual components, they are often a very good deal. If you buy passive speakers, while you may not get the same sound quality, you can get a decent system with a smaller price tag.

## Components, connections, load, and efficiency

These are the four items you will need to deal with when buying speakers. The first is components. In our case this is really about the size, number, and type, not quality (although buying a brand known for quality will help ensure you get something decent). Most entry-level PA cabinets are known as *2-way enclosures*, meaning they devote two components to reproducing different parts of the sonic spectrum. Most often, these will consist of a large speaker called a woofer and a high-frequency driver attached to a horn. Let's look at woofers first.

A *woofer* in a two-way enclosure comes most often in one of two sizes—12" or 15". For smaller systems you can get 10" and even 8" woofers. The larger the speaker, the more air it moves and the better it generally is at reproducing low frequencies. Which you choose is largely a function of usage and taste. If you are running keys or bass through the mains a 15 is likely better, while some sound people will tell you that a 12 is better for vocals.

The horn driver reproduces the high frequencies and comes in a couple of flavors—compression drivers and piezo drivers (although most companies have stopped using piezo drivers and gone to the more "pro" compression driver). The horn is a device that both acts like the cone on a speaker (it vibrates and creates sound) and aims the high-frequency sound. The shape of the horn will determine in large part the dispersion of sound in the room. Your best bet is for a fairly wide dispersion horn—just ask about the horn's "throw" when buying a speaker, to make sure you are not getting something too specialized.

The next thing you need to look at is the cabinet's *load*. Any device in an electrical circuit impedes the flow of electricity to some degree. This impedance is expressed in *ohms*, and when you are looking at speakers, the lower the impedance, the more actual power you will get out of your amps. But be careful! If you go too low (say, under 4 ohms), you stand a very good chance of blowing up your amps.

Most PA cabinets present a nominal load of 8 ohms, but if you run two of them on the same amp channel (or with a mono power amp) you get a load of 4 ohms, not 16. If you want to know how the math works, just remember that when you are "daisy-chaining" speaker cabs, the total impedance is figured by multiplying the loads of each cabinet and then dividing that number by the sum of the loads of all cabinets in the chain—in the case of two 8-ohm cabinets it looks like this: (8x8)/(8+8) or 64/16=4. But if you don't want to tax your brain that much, just remember that two 8-ohm enclosures will give you a 4-ohm load. Do not go below 4 ohms, and you will be okay. Check the enclosures you are using, and make sure they are 8-ohm cabinets, as there are some enclosures that present a 4-ohm load, and combining two of them will get you to the 2-ohm point, which can be dangerous.

*Efficiency* refers to how much sound a speaker produces for the amount of power it takes in. The higher the number in an efficiency rating, the better. This rating is expressed in terms of *decibels* or *dB*. A three-decibel difference in efficiency can make a huge difference in the amount of sound a cabinet produces and how much power that cabinet needs from the amp. A reasonable efficiency rating for an entry level PA cabinet is in the 96-98 dB range.

Finally, we come to connections. In a passive cabinet, you will likely find one of two kinds of connectors: a ¼" plug similar to what you see on a guitar amp, or a more professional connector known as either a *Speakon* or *twist-lock*. See photo on the following page.

The advantages of the Speakon over the ¼" plug are numerous, including the fact that it can safely carry more current from the amp to the speaker and the fact that it locks into its jack, making it all but impossible for some drunk bar patron to trip over a cable and unplug it from the cabinet. (It does, however, make it more likely that the same drunk tripping over the same cable will fall on his or her face or even pull the speaker cabinet down onto themselves!)

**Standard Speakon plug.**

Up until fairly recently, almost all PA cabinets had ¼" connectors and, especially if you buy your first PA used, you may end up with them still. The most important thing to keep in mind if you are using this kind of connector is that you should never use a guitar or instrument cable to go between a power amp and speakers. Shielded instrument cables are constructed very differently from speaker cable. Without getting too technical, just know that a shielded cable used in this application will make it impossible to get anywhere close to optimum performance from your system.

## Monitors

These are typically smaller speaker cabinets that are pointed back at the band, to allow the players to hear themselves and each other so they can play together effectively. Monitors come in a number of different formats, including the increasingly popular ear-based or personal monitors of both the wired and wireless variety. While the price of these units has come down considerably in the past couple of years, they are still more of an investment than you are likely to make on a first PA.

This leaves us with two basic types of monitors: the standard wedge and the less common but often effective mic stand-mounted *spot* monitor. Both spot and wedge monitors come in powered and passive versions. Each connects to your system the same way: The output of a monitor or aux send (more on this in the section on mixers) goes to a power amp and then to the monitors. In the case of powered monitors, the amp is built in, so the signal goes straight from the mixer to the monitor.

Another approach that Quint once used is *side monitoring*. The band used its practice PA system as the monitor system for big gigs and set it on the sides of the stage, pointing inward toward the band. This also worked well as fills for the audience at the front of the stage. (This was generally for larger venues with capacities of as many as 1,000 people.)

All of the same considerations used in choosing main speakers also apply to monitors.

**Typical wedge monitor.**

**Typical stand-mounted spot monitor.**

Now that we have covered the beginning and end of the sound chain, let's get into the middle section of mixers, processors, and amps. We followed this somewhat convoluted order because, as you will see, you have a number of options for combining parts of this middle section with powered mixers, mixers with built-in processing, and even powered speakers. We will start by explaining the individual components and then look at the combo choices.

## Mixers

From the mic, the signal or sound goes on to the mixer. This is where all of the inputs are combined and "tweaked" before the end result goes to the speakers (and the audience). Let's look at a typical gigging mixer.

**Inputs.** Where the signal arrives to the mixer. Inputs are generally one of a couple of types. *Mic inputs* have an XLR (three-pin) jack and a mic preamp built into the circuit to bring the fairly weak signal from a mic up to a level the mixer can deal with. *Line inputs* are generally ¼" style and used for a stronger "line level" signal, including those from keyboards or drum machines. In a stereo mixer, some channels will take two inputs; known as *stereo channels*, these are basically two channels with shared tone controls and a shared volume control. Mic input channels will often have both XLR and ¼" jacks; these are known as mic/line channels.

**Trim.** The next step in the chain. Trim basically controls the output of the preamp for a channel. The idea is to get as much signal as possible into the channel without overloading it, which would result in distortion. A mic level signal will require more level at the trim control than a line level signal.

**EQ.** Short for equalization. This is similar to the bass and treble controls on your stereo at home. The most important things to remember about EQ are that a little twist of a knob can accomplish a lot and that it is always better to cut than it is to boost.

**Aux sends.** Think of these as detours in the signal path within the channel. ("Aux" is short for auxiliary.) There are two types of aux sends: pre-fader and post-fader, generally referred to as just pre and post sends. A pre-fader send is not affected by any changes made by the main fader to the overall level of a channel, while a post-fader send *is* affected by the same moves. Pre-fader sends are generally used to send signal for a separate monitor mix while post-fader sends are most often used to send signal to a reverb unit or other effects processor.

**Fader.** This sets the overall level of a channel without affecting the level of the other channels on a mixer. From the fader, the signal goes to the mixer's master output section.

**Master section.** Where the final levels are determined prior to moving on to any outboard processors and then on to power amps. The master section will generally include level controls for master output as well as return levels for those post-fader sends. (These control how much of the detoured signal is returned to the master mix.) You will also get a master level control for the pre-fader sends, which will control overall monitor level.

## Power amps

Let's start with the most important thing to understand: A power amp and a guitar amp are not the same thing. A power amp typically has no tone controls, just volume. They exist only to increase the power of the signal coming from the mixer to something strong enough to drive the speakers.

Power ratings are expressed in watts at a specific ohm load. (Remember, we talked about impedance when we discussed speakers.) When comparing amps, you need to look at the power levels at the same ohm load as that provided by your speakers—if you are running 8-ohm loads, does it really matter what the power rating of an amp is at 4 ohms?

Before we get further into power levels, let's look at impedance one more time. As you shop, you will see lots of manufacturers claiming very high power ratings based on a 2-ohm load. We strongly recommend that you ignore those ratings as: 1) it is unlikely you will ever set up in a manner that will get you a 2-ohm load; 2) that impedance level is often dangerous and can easily result in a blown amp; and 3) even if you were to set up with a 2-ohm load, most places where you will be playing simply cannot provide the amount of electrical current you would need to get the power that any amp claims at two ohms. Two-ohm ratings are fine in theory but rarely have anything to do with real-life gigging.

Power ratings can be tricky on another level as well. Not so long ago, almost all amp companies published power ratings using a standard called RMS. (It means "root mean squared" and, trust us, it's more math than you really want to deal with.) But go into any music store today and you will see a plethora of rating schemes that include continuous, program, peak, burst, and sometimes even the old standby RMS. Engineers debate endlessly over which method is best, but that doesn't help the average musician walking into a store to buy a power amp.

Truth is that these different rating schemes, and especially the emergence of the 2-ohm rating, are mostly about marketing. Too many manufacturers have joined the race (though some of the better, old-line companies have done so quite unwillingly) to put the highest possible wattage rating on the box, figuring that most musicians will buy a power amp based on the most power for the price.

All of this creates a problem for the average musician.

About all we can tell you is this: When comparing specs make sure it's an "apples to apples" comparison. Check out the reviews magazines and ask other giggers and sound techs what they like. Finally, try to buy a brand with a reputation for quality and durability.

One last issue on power amps: connections. Power amps have connections at the input and output, and both of these can come in a number of flavors. Input connections are usually ¼" phone connectors or balanced XLR, although some amps aimed more at the DJ market will have RCA connectors like the ones on your home stereo. Outputs have more variety, including ¼", Speakon, banana plugs, and binding posts.

We all have our preferences in connectors, but what you really need to be concerned with is making sure that you have the proper cables or at least adapters for the amp and speakers. A number of years ago, before Speakon connectors became common in the gigging market,

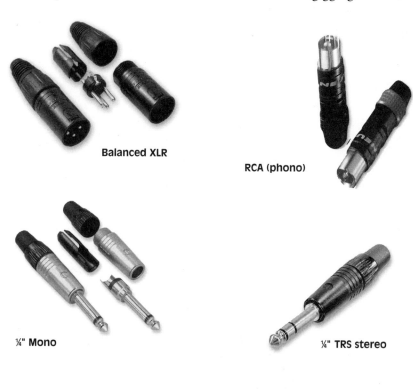

**Balanced XLR**

**RCA (phono)**

**¼" Mono**

**¼" TRS stereo**

Bill went to a gig with a new power amp he was testing out. When he got everything set up and was ready to wire the speakers to the amp, he was confronted with the choice between an unfamiliar connector that refused to admit his standard ¼" speaker cable plug or a set of binding posts. He learned an expensive lesson when, with time for downbeat rapidly approaching, he had to cut the ends off of his speaker cables in order to wire them into the binding posts. He now carries ¼"-to-banana plugs and a couple of other adapters in case of a similar surprise.

### Outboard gear

This is kind of like the options on a car. Outboard gear provides "services" that range in importance from crucial to convenient but often do not come as part of the basic package. You can divide this gear into four basic groups: dynamics processors, EQ, effects, and speaker management.

*Dynamics processors* refer to compressors, limiters, and noise gates. As the term "dynamics" implies, all of these devices deal with the volume of a signal in one form or another. Compressors and limiters "squash" the dynamic range of any signal passed through them. This means that the volume of a signal is not allowed to go above or below a set point. Learning how to run a compressor is beyond the scope of this book, but let us just say that a threshold is set, or the point at which the compressor "kicks in," and attack and release times are set to determine how strongly the compressor "grabs" and "lets go of" the signal. Finally, the amount or "ratio" of compression is determined. A noise gate is more of an on-off switch for a signal based on its strength—below a set point, the signal path is closed and the sound is "off," and it opens or turns on when the signal reaches a preset point. Generally, compressors are used to "smooth out" your sound (although be aware that compression should be subtle and that over-compressing is both easy and sounds terrible), while gates are used to eliminate low-level noise when there is no signal being passed through the system, or to keep certain mics "off" when they are not in actual use. This is most common on things like drum mics.

As we discussed earlier, EQ is basically an extended tone control. Outboard EQs are generally used to adjust to any acoustic deficiencies of the venue or to control feedback. EQs come in two basic flavors: graphic and parametric. *Graphic EQs* are so named because they look like a graph, with sliders for a range of frequencies that can be boosted or cut from the center "0" point. They come in various configurations, ranging from five to 31 bands of EQ.

**A typical graphic EQ.**

**A typical parametric EQ.**

A *parametric EQ* is something you will likely not deal with at this level, but it generally consists of three controls: *frequency*, which determines the center point of the sonic area to be adjusted; *Q*, which determines the width of that area, or how many frequencies above and below the center point are affected by any adjustment; and *level*, which determines the amount of boost or cut of the specified frequencies.

The one exception to the "parametrics are for pros" rule is a specialized kind of EQ known as a *feedback killer*. These devices "listen" to the signal, searching for that awful squeal we call acoustic feedback. When that squeal occurs, the feedback killer determines the offending frequency and knocks it way down via a parametric EQ with a very narrow Q. Some graphic EQs perform much the same function, with an LED lighting above the slider that controls the frequency range where the feedback occurs, so that the operator can bring it down manually.

Our next category is the *effects processor*. These devices range from units that only do reverb to multi-effect units that can do two, three, or even four effects at once. An effects processor generally takes its input signal from a post-fader aux send on the board and returns it to the mix via either an unused channel or a master effects return.

Most use the master effects return, although using an otherwise open channel (or pair of channels in the case of a stereo device) does give you the added flexibility of being able to EQ the reverb or delayed or otherwise affected signal in addition to determining its overall strength in relation to the "dry" or unaffected signal.

Finally, we have *speaker management*, which refers to devices like crossovers that are used to allow a speaker to work as efficiently as possible. At the gigging band level—especially for bands that are just buying their first or second PA—crossovers are built into the speaker enclosure. If the speaker is passive, then so is the crossover. A powered speaker will generally use an active crossover, which divides the signal into highs and lows and sends each to its own amp before going on to the speakers. You can use an active crossover with passive speakers, but it means buying more amps and cabinets that are set up for bi-amping. When you are getting started with sound, this is probably an area best left to the pros. In other words, go with what's built in until you get a real feel for live sound.

## Mix and match, or all in one?

When buying your first PA there are a couple of systems to consider. The first is made up of separate components—that is, a mixer, an amp, and processors all separate. The other is some kind of combo system, where one piece of gear takes the place of two or more components.

Up until the recent emergence of powered speakers, the combo approach meant a powered mixer. Though that is now just one possible approach, we'll start there as it is still the most common way to begin learning live sound.

A powered mixer combines the functions of a mixer and power amp and often those of an effects processor as well. Don't let sound people with a lot of experience convince you that all powered mixers suck. Yes, for a long time buying a powered mixer meant compromising in both the mixer and amp segments of your system. But over the past few years, Carvin, EV, Mackie, Yamaha, Yorkville, and other reputable companies have been making powered mixers that sound very good and have all the features most bands need, including digital effects. Some of these mixers include three or even four power amps, allowing you to run both mains and monitors without buying another amp.

The one thing to be aware of when buying a powered mixer is the number of patch points available on the mixer. That is, are there places in the signal path where you can "break in" and add additional power or processing? At the very least there should be a set of ins and outs between the mixer and amp portions and at least one monitor or aux send. The break-in at the power amp point will allow you to upgrade to a larger power amp or go to a powered speaker system as your needs grow without having to immediately buy a new mixer.

The other combo approach is to buy a passive mixer and powered speakers. Given the large number of passive mixers that include good onboard effects, this is a great approach that means buying just two types of gear. Price-wise, buying a powered mixer and speakers is likely a bit less expensive than a good passive mixer and powered speakers.

For a collection of helpful PA tips from various PA manufacturers, go to www.covergigs.com. Now that you have your personal gear together and have a sound system, it's time to get all that gear to the gig and set it up—so you can actually play for a real, live audience.

## TECH 4

## SET UP, SOUND CHECK, AND THE GIG

*If you can't hear everyone else in the band, then you're too loud! Good stage balance goes a long way toward a good sound out front.*

Mark Legault

The preparation is done and now it's time for the payoff—the gig. Notice that we didn't say that the *work* is done. Yes, the gig is the pay-off, and the time spent playing in front of an enthusiastic audience can be some of the best time of your life, but that doesn't mean the work is done. Example: As this book was being finished Bill did a regular bar gig at a place 15 minutes away from his home. He started packing up gear at about 3:30 p.m. on a Friday. After packing up, loading up, unloading, setting up, playing four sets, tearing down, packing up, driving home, and unloading, he got home and in bed at 3:30 a.m. on Saturday morning. Don't ever let anyone tell you this isn't work.

In this chapter we'll walk through the technical aspects of setup, sound check, and doing a gig. Because there are other books and materials that intensely cover sound and mixing, we'll focus on some of the more practical matters that these technical books tend to brush over.

### Loading in and setting up

This is the point where you can either make or break the gig. A smooth setup without any glitches, tension, or headaches is one of the best ways to guarantee a good gig. And the best way to make it smooth is to stay organized. It is pretty amazing to watch most bands try to get set up. It is a band. These people know how to work together, at least in theory. But when it comes to getting gear loaded in and set up, it often seems that not only are the band members not working together, they are actually trying to make things hard for everyone but themselves.

So who goes first? This is perhaps the most important thing to determine up front. What we are trying to avoid here is a situation where·everyone is tripping over each other trying to get *their* stuff on stage. If the sound system is being provided by the venue, then—after the soundman gives you the go ahead—get the gear that takes the longest to set up in first. This will usually be the drums, and this is a good place to start as most stage setups are wrapped around the drums anyway.

If you are providing the sound system, then without exception the PA gets loaded in and set up first. This is not just because it is generally the most complicated part of the setup. PA systems involve running a lot of cables—mic cables, speaker cables, etc.—and one of the worst things you can do is get into a situation where you are trying to route long cable runs around, over, under, or through someone else's gear. Get the gear in, the speakers and monitors placed, and all cable run before anything else is allowed on the stage.

There is another bonus to this method if you are the one running the PA. In this case, if you allow the rest of the band to set up at the same time that you are trying to get the PA up and running, not only do you make your job harder, but you virtually guarantee that no one else in the band will help at all with the PA setup. It is almost a natural law that most band members will try to get out of helping with this task. It's just one of those things.

This method also helps you to stay organized as you move into the part of the evening known as sound check.

*I've had plenty of sound-checking adventures, from absolute nightmares to euphoric experiences. The most important tip: Make friends with the sound tech! He or she has ultimate control over your gig, so don't piss 'em off.*

Debra Davis
*Bandleader and singer, magazine columnist*

## Sound check basics

Sound check may just be the most important part of your gig. It is also the part that is most often shortchanged or even ignored both by pros and beginners.

Let's start by defining a sound check. There are a couple of kinds, the very basic being a *line check*, where the only goal is to make sure that all mics and other inputs are actually working and that signal is getting to the mains and monitors. Though this is not a "real" sound check, it is all you will often get. (The rest of the sound check then takes place during the first couple of songs.)

A real sound check will involve not only the line check but also adjusting individual inputs for tone and putting everything together into a good mix for both mains and monitors. The main thing to remember during a sound check is that this is not performance/jamming/warming-up time. If the sound tech wants to hear just the kick drum for what seems like an eternity, that doesn't make it okay for the guitarist to work on his latest speed-metal riffs at full volume because he is bored. Pay attention. Do what you're told. Be cooperative. It will help you to have a better gig.

The hardest question to answer when it comes to sound checks is when to do one. In a perfect world (or a well-paying Union gig...), sound check will be scheduled for at least a couple and likely several hours before the actual gig. But chances are that your situation is different.

In most new working bands ... in the vast majority of *all* working bands ... most if not all of the players will have day jobs or be in school. This means that you are always rushed, rarely arrive to the gig more than an hour or so before you are scheduled to play, and will almost never have the time for a leisurely sound check.

So if you are providing the PA, you need to do what we call *first-tune sound checks*. Even with some venues that provide the PA, you will not get a real sound check because—this is especially true of restaurants and sports bars—they don't want the patrons to have to listen to you dialing in your sound. Here is how a first-tune sound check works:

Let's start with a scenario that assumes you have someone running the sound for you. You will need to have done a quick and dirty line check to make sure everything is working. Next, you need to have a song in your set that starts with just a few people and builds as the song goes on. Bill's band often uses Cannonball Adderley's "Mercy, Mercy, Mercy" because the band specializes in classic soul and R&B. The trick is to find a song like this that fits in with the kind of music you play.

Starting out this way has two purposes. First, it gives the sound tech a chance to give a few seconds of attention to each instrument as it comes in rather than having to deal with everything at once. Second, it keeps you from hitting the audience with a blaring bad mix and making a catastrophic first impression.

## Communicating with and hiring a sound tech

One of the best ways to make sure you get the most out of sound check is to communicate well with the sound tech. Unfortunately, communication between musicians and sound engineers is often dicey at best. This is because we seem to speak different languages. A musician may say that a sound is too "crunchy," while a sound tech will likely say that the low mids are overemphasized. Because the engineer—whether someone the band has hired or someone who works for the venue—has his or her hands on the knobs, it is best that you learn to communicate at least to some degree in Techspeak. Here are some basics courtesy of Nashville sound hound Gordon Jennings, has mixed for name artists including Take 6 and Willie Nelson.

Know your frequencies. Don't ask for more highs when you really want high mids. Likewise, don't ask for lows when you mean low mids.

This is the most basic exchange between an engineer and a musician, and lucidity here cannot be emphasized enough. A good engineer should be able to translate such phrases as "boxy" or "harsh" or "sparkle," but you should try to avoid such terms, nonetheless. This will help you as well, since the more specific you are, the better the results will be. Play with an equalizer in your rehearsal studio and learn where these ranges of frequencies are.

That being said, if you get too specific the engineer might think you are trying to tell him how to do his job — which is a bad thing. Besides, they usually know the room better than you do. "One night this artist kept saying, 'Put more 5kHz in the house' and demanding I set it up 'his way'," says Terry Messal, house mixer at LA's Genghis Cohen. "He didn't know my room, and when I EQ'd it like that it sounded lousy."

Steve Folsom is a Boston-based engineer who has mixed for some pretty big names. He says: "Trying to call out specific frequencies is an admirable quest, but it is usually problematic. Two people will probably have different versions of what they perceive 2K to be."

Next, know some basic audio terms. *EQ* means equalizer, of course. *Mic* means microphone. *DI* means direct input or direct interface, which is a little box used to take inputs directly from the source, usually used on keyboards and bass guitar. *Signal* means the sound in electronic form, usually within the console or any external device. *Strip* means input channel on a mixer. *Gain* means amplification of a signal, or raising the electronic level of a signal, although sometimes when more acoustic volume is needed it is likewise called gain or level. *Amplitude* is a measure of gain; the greater the level, the greater the amplitude. *Reverb*, short for "reverberation," means the product of a unit that duplicates an acoustic environment, such as a concert hall or room. A "*dry*" signal can sound like it is inside a hall or room or such with the use of these; an effected signal is sometimes referred to as "*wet*." *Grease* is another term for reverb. *Echo*, sometimes mistaken for reverb, is something else altogether. Echo, or *Slap*, is a distinct repeat or series of repetitions of the original signal, like yelling "hello" into a canyon. Echo and reverb are not interchangeable, as many seem to think. Once again, it is important to be specific in what you ask for. Don't ask for echo when you want reverb, or vice versa.

*AC* is alternating current, the stuff you get when you plug into the wall. *DC* is direct current, the stuff you get from a battery. A *power supply* is a device that changes AC to DC; you can find one in every piece of electronic gear. *Solid state* means transistors as opposed to tubes. *Distortion* is any difference between the signal at the output compared to the input. This can be good or bad, intentional or accidental. Most guitar players use distortion to add bite to their sound. For that matter, technically speaking, any signal that has reverb (or is even compressed) is distorted, yet these are good distortions. Bad distortion such as overdriving an input channel so the red "clip" light is on most of the time is quite unpleasant to the ear, as we all know. Because the peaks of the signal are cut off, this is referred to as *clipping*. Blown speakers or power amps can cause distortion as well.

### Frequency basics

The basic rules for EQ are simple and come, once again, from Gordon Jennings:

Trust your ears. Listen for anything ugly and get rid of it. The easiest way of doing this is to boost sliders on the graphic, since it's easier to identify ugly by exaggerating it. Once you find the ugliness, cut it.

Special notes on certain frequencies: Any 2" horn will resonate at 2.5kHz , low-end boom is generally about 160Hz, and muddiness is usually around 250Hz. Plus, I always cut 4Hz just because I don't like it, and 8kHz because that's the awful brain-dart region. Loud does not need to hurt.

Vocal intelligibility can be enhanced with a small boost in the midrange, usually 1 to 4kHz, and presence with high end added at 12 to 16kHz. This may give you a problem with cymbal leakage on a small stage, so be careful. Kick drum likes 40 to 60Hz added and low mids cut, around 250Hz. Definition between kick and bass guitar can be established by boosting those same low mids on the bass guitar. Remember, 310Hz is the bass player's frequency. Every other instrument will be a matter of individual taste. Once again, trust your ears.

Perhaps the most important thing in the live mix is the musical arrangement. It all begins onstage. To maintain sonic distance between instruments, it is crucial that they don't all play in the same register. If two instruments are playing the same note at the same time, the brain hears only the one played louder; this is due to *psycho-acoustics*.

The two basic rules of the live mix are: 1) make everything sound good; and 2) make it so you can hear everything. That may seem simple, but remember, if it's not happening onstage, it won't happen in the house. Be clever, be good, but keep it open! Think "air" when you arrange your material.

Speaking of sonic distance, a stereo system is always better than a mono one and should be utilized. Pan stuff. Keep the middle open for the vocals. That way you won't be fighting with levels, trying to make everything louder than everything else. Got a stereo guitar rig? Pan it hard. Remember your psycho-acoustics, and keep only the things in the middle that won't interfere with the vocals.

## Do it yourself ... or not?

So now you understand the basic terms and are familiar with what frequencies are what, but the question remains: Do you do the sound yourself or hire a band soundperson? There is no right answer to this question; there are too many variables. If there is a player in the band who is largely stationary and who is not doing a lot of singing, then having that person run sound from the stage is a perfectly legit choice. But beware the "doing-too-much" syndrome. Both of your *humble* authors have fallen into this trap. We both play, we both sing, we have both tried too often to add sound duties to that. It is hard enough to maintain the focus to do two jobs (playing and singing or playing and running sound); adding a third means something suffers, and when that something is either your performance or your overall sound, then it is an unacceptable compromise.

Especially when you are starting out, we strongly recommend that you have a soundperson to both run the sound and help set up and strike the system. Think of this person as another band member, as crucial to your show as your drummer. This doesn't mean that you have to hire a pro. You're starting out, right? It's no sin to have a soundperson who is coming up right along with you. Find a friend who wants to be "a part of the band" but who doesn't play. Teach him or her how to set up the system and run it. We both have a ton of respect for real pro audio guys and would never want anyone to think that we are saying it is the kind of thing that doesn't require training and talent. It does. But the basics can be pretty easily learned.

## Mixing from the stage

Yes, you should have someone mixing the sound from a position where they can actually hear things. But the sad truth is that you will often need to have someone in the band do it from the stage. This can work (in fact, a few years ago Prince did an entire tour mixing his own sound from a console located backstage), but it means some real compromise and knowing the pitfalls so you can avoid them.

Okay, let's get real: Mixing from the stage sucks. But it is unfortunately the most common situation you will encounter. It is impossible to really hear the house mix from the stage, so you have to keep some basic rules in mind.

**Carry your own console.** You are already in a difficult situation; no sense making it worse by getting stuck with unfamiliar tools.

**Keep the stage volume down.** High stage volume levels create a number of problems, the most serious being that they make it difficult to impossible to hear one another. Mixing from the stage means that everyone in the band has to help keep the mix right by not blowing away everyone else onstage. Guitar players are the biggest offenders. I know that a Marshall sounds better cranked than it does on "2"—so buy a power-soak.

**Make one band member the sound tech.** Although everyone needs to cooperate, there has to be a point person who is responsible for the sound. That person should be the one to make the adjustments and deal with any problems. This person also needs to have the trust of everyone else onstage; if he or she tells you to turn down, do it!

**Get someone off the stage and into the house.** Arrange all of your sets so that there are a couple of points where one band member can leave the stage and check out the sound in the house. Maybe you have a lead singer who takes a break while the bass player sings a couple of songs per set. Maybe you have a horn player who can sit out the occasional tune. On those songs, send the unoccupied party into the house to check things out and either make the adjustments or report to the person in charge of the board.

**Keep it simple.** In most cases when you are mixing from the stage, it is best to put as little through the PA as possible—vocals, horns, maybe some drums. The rest of the band can rely on their own amps. This will give you a somewhat better idea of the house sound from the stage. It will also make it easier to make adjustments.

### Ten tips for better sound

Whether you have a soundperson or are doing it yourself from the stage, the basics are the same. Here are ten additional tips to finish off this chapter.

**1. A great mix starts at the bottom,** which means drums and bass. Spend a good deal of your time getting those right. Use plenty of pillow or packing for the kick drum. An additional drum tip: Fly cymbals low because you'll rarely have the luxury of overhead drum mics; they'll be more likely to be picked up by the hi-hat or tom mic. (This strategy will also help conserve your drummer's energy.)

**2. Louder is not better.** Maximum gain is not the goal. The goal is tonality. One of the biggest mistakes we see is the soundperson trying just to get it loud. Remember that most audience members really don't enjoy their ears bleeding.

**3. It's about the overall sound.** Most musicians selfishly put so much effort and focus into their individual sound that they have little time or mental space left for the complete band sound. If each band member would put a little more effort into the band's sound as a whole, it will pay off exponentially. As Nashville-based engineer John Guertin says, "Your instrument is not the most important one on the stage."

**4. Learn about gain structure.** It is more tech than we can really get into here, but there are a number of places to find out about it, including at least three features in *Gig* magazine over the past few years. In sum, "There's no such thing as gain for free. If it's screwed up at the beginning (of the sound chain), it's going to be screwed up at the end," says live sound engineer Kevin Sims.

**5. Vocals belong on top.** Anything that is louder than the singer is too loud. So focus your mix on the vocals. The main vocal melody and harmonies are what audiences are going to relate to most. If they can't hear the vocal melody and harmonies, they won't think your band is very good. Vocals are king. (So, yes, tell your guitar player to turn down!)

**6. A little reverb goes a long way.** "No amount of processing is ever going to make it sound better," says Sims.

**7. Ditto compression.**

**8. With EQ, subtraction is better than addition.** Do your first sound check with the master or outboard EQ in the out position. Get the room sounding as good as possible without any EQ; then subtract from there. And don't get in the lazy habit of leaving your EQ set up exactly the same way from gig to gig and from room to room.

**9. It is at least as important for you to hear yourself as it is for the audience to hear you.** Good monitors count. "You have to start onstage. If you don't have a good stage sound, you're not going to have a good house sound," says Guertin. So if you can't afford a killer stage monitor system, or you're not playing large, loud rooms, don't be afraid sometimes to set up the mains behind the mic line. It really builds confidence and coherence when players can hear exactly what the audience is hearing. (Although it makes feedback much more likely, so be careful and keep the volume low.)

**10. The more complex your system, the more likely it is that something will go wrong.** "Make sure you're not overdriving any portion of the system at any time," says Sims. So especially when you are mixing yourself, keep the system as simple as possible. You have plenty of other things to worry about.

## You're on your own

So you're backstage, waiting. They audience is cheering for more. They're clapping in unison—500 people wanting you to play another song. They want an encore. Yes, an encore from you—a lowly cover band. You step out on to the stage to the cheers and rip into Chuck Berry's classic "Johnny B. Goode." Who'd-a thought that this could ever happen? Certainly not you in those early rehearsal sessions, when you thought you were going to throw up because the band sounded so bad. But you made it. After all that work you're in a pro band that is working regularly—making money making music. Knowing how to set up and use your PA system is the final step in learning what it takes to be in a successful cover band—or any band for that matter. By following the tips and techniques we've outlined in this book, you can and will get to this point in your career. It doesn't matter whether it's "as far as you will go" or whether it's a stepping stone to "the big time." It will always be fulfilling and a heck of a lot of fun.

But hey, wake up. You're not there yet. It's 5:45 on a Friday evening—time to load the truck and get on the road to your first gig.

For more information on everything in this book, visit our web site at www.covergigs.com.

## ACKNOWLEDGMENTS

First we thank our wives, who put up with not seeing us much for the many months it took to put this project together. Next, thanks to the group of working musicians to whom we turned to for advice and ideas throughout the process. The quotes you read that lead off most of the chapters came from this group of folks.

A big thanks as well to the *Gig* writers whose work is featured throughout the book: Mark Amundson, Bruce Bartlett, Dave Beyer, Ken Biedzynski, Bill Churchville, Debra Davis, Steve Eason, Cheryl Evans, Dave Howard, Gordon Jennings, Billy Mitchell, Riley Wilson, and others who may not have been directly quoted but whose efforts have taught us much about this business over the years.

Thanks to Jack Nelson, Quint's journalism professor many years ago at BYU, where the idea for this book was born.

Thanks to Dan Whitley, the agent who gave us both our first serious paying gigs (in competing bands) and started us on the path to being professional musicians. But most important, thanks to all our fellow band mates in the myriad bands over the years.

## ABOUT THE AUTHORS

Now a faculty member at Brigham Young University, **Quint Randle** has been a working musician, songwriter, and journalist for more than 25 years. He has played everywhere from coffeehouses in the Midwest to the Bluebird Cafe in Nashville to rock clubs on the Sunset Strip. He founded *Gig* magazine in 1986 after graduating from BYU with a degree in journalism. Since then  he has also founded several other national publications and produced instructional videos as well as a TV show for ESPN2. He holds a master's degree in communications from Pepperdine and a doctorate in mass media from Michigan State. His latest cover gig was as lead singer and rhythm guitarist for the Beagles. Several publishing companies have signed his songs recently as well.

The editor of the live sound magazine *Front of House* and former editor of *Gig*, **Bill Evans** has been a working journalist for the better part of two decades and a working musician for the better part of three. In fact, except for a couple of years spent living in southern  Chile, Bill has been in working bands constantly since 1975. Over the past two decades he has been fronting an R&B dance band called Rev. Bill and the Soul Believers, working every kind of gig you can imagine, from corporate parties and large festivals to some of the worst dives in Southern California. He has been honored both as a writer and editor by the California Newspaper Publishers Association.

## PHOTO CREDITS

# INDEX